INTIMACY WITH CHRIST

FAITHESSENTIALS

Other Titles in the FaithEssentials Series

The Pursuit of God by A.W. Tozer

Sit, Walk, Stand by Watchman Nee

The Calvary Road by Roy Hession

Acceptable Sacrifice by John Bunyan

Other Books by James N. Watkins

The Imitation of Christ: Classic Devotions in Today's Language

Overcoming Fear and Worry

God, I Don't Understand: Unanswered Prayer, Unfulfilled Promises, Unpunished Evil

Squeezing Good Out of Bad

JAMES N. WATKINS
EDITOR

INTIMACY WITH CHRIST

Classic Devotions by
BROTHER LAWRENCE, FRANCIS of
ASSISI, TERESA of AVILA, and Others

FAITHESSENTIALS

CLC PUBLICATIONS
Fort Washington, PA 19034

Intimacy with Christ
FaithEssentials Edition
Published by CLC Publications

U.S.A.
P.O. Box 1449, Fort Washington, PA 19034

UNITED KINGDOM
CLC International (UK)
Unit 5, Glendale Avenue, Sandycroft, Flintshire, CH5 2QP

Printed in the United States of America

ISBN (paperback): 978-1-61958-326-9
ISBN (e-book): 978-1-61958-327-6

Italics in Scripture quotations are the emphasis of the author.

Other devotions, paraphrased in modern language, are from various sources, listed at the end of this book.

To Elsie Drummonds

who lived out an intimate relationship
with Christ for all to see

Contents

Preface

Then Christ will make his home in your hearts as you trust in him. Your roots will grow down into God's love and keep you strong. And may you have the power to understand, as all God's people should, how wide, how long, how high, and how deep his love is. May you experience the love of Christ, though it is too great to understand fully. Then you will be made complete with all the fullness of life and power that comes from God.

Ephesians 3:17–19

Most churches do very well in sharing information and fairly well in providing opportunities for involvement. However, according to Willow Creek Association network of thousands of churches, "63 percent of the most active and committed church members are so discouraged with church and its ability to support their faith that they are considering leaving the church." I believe what's missing is intimacy with Christ.

Jesus reveals the purpose of the church in His last earthly prayer: "I pray that they will all be one, just as you and I are one—as you are in me, Father, and I am in you. And may they be in us so that the world will believe you sent me" (John 17:21).

As a Pharisee, the apostle Paul excelled in information. Jewish children—both boys and girls—began the study of the Torah, the first five books of the Bible, at age five. At ten, they were expected to master the Mishnah, the interpretations of the Torah, and at fifteen to be able to make Rabbinic interpretations of the Law. The brightest students went on to Beth Midrash, "graduate school," under the instruction of the best rabbis. Paul boasts that he studied under Gamaliel, one of the most honored rabbis of the time (see Acts 5:34, 22:3).

Memorization was an important part of education, so like most high-ranking Pharisees, Paul probably had memorized all five books of the Law. That's a lot of information.

And as far as involvement in religious activity, Pharisees fasted two days a week and tithed not only money but produce, down to the last mint leaf; they kept all 613 laws of the Torah, as well as hundreds of so-called "fence laws," designed to prevent the devoted from trespassing the laws of Moses.

So, as far as information and involvement, Paul could proclaim:

> Indeed, if others have reason for confidence in their own efforts, I have even more!

> I was circumcised when I was eight days old. I am a pure-blooded citizen of Israel and a member of the tribe of Benjamin—a real Hebrew if there ever was one! I was a member of the Pharisees, who demand the strictest obedience to the Jewish law. I was so zealous that I harshly persecuted the church. And as for righteousness, I obeyed the law without fault. (Phil. 3:4–6)

But the apostle continues:

> I once thought these things were valuable, but now I consider them worthless because of what Christ has done. Yes, everything else is worthless when compared with the infinite value of knowing Christ Jesus my Lord. For his sake I have discarded everything else, counting it all as garbage, so that I could gain Christ and become one with him. I no longer count on my own righteousness through obeying the law; rather, I become righteous through faith in Christ. For God's way of making us right with himself depends on faith. (3:7–9)

Without intimacy with Christ, all the information and involvement for Him may result in our hearing, "I never knew you. Get away from me, you who break God's laws" (Matt. 7:23).

During the Middle Ages, a group of Christians desired to know Christ and His presence in all areas of life. Like many churches today, information and involvement were the main emphases of the church of the time—with little intimacy. Rote memorization of the Ten Commandments, the Lord's Prayer, and the Apostle's Creed often took the place of a living relationship with Christ.

In a previous book, I introduced readers to the writing of Thomas à Kempis and his classic book, *The Imitation of Christ*. This collection of devotionals follows the same format with excerpts from some of the most popular writers of that time—who are still revered today by Protestants and Catholics alike. Let me introduce you to these classic devotional writers who were passionate about experiencing intimacy with Christ.

Anonymous (Late fourteenth century)
This unknown writer ironically wrote *The Cloud of Unknowing*. The title derives from the belief that God is beyond human knowledge and wisdom. From internal evidence, it appears he was an English monk devoted to a cloistered, contemplative life. He is also credited for writing three lesser known works including *An Epistle on Prayer*.

Bernard of Clairvaux (1090–1153)
Bernard founded and oversaw over 160 Cistercian monasteries, which emphasized manual labor and self-sufficiency by supporting themselves through agriculture and other businesses. Education and academic pursuits were also emphasized, but primarily *lectio*

divina. This method of praying while contemplating the Word did not treat Scripture as a mere book to be studied but as the "living Word" intended to transform the reader's life. This inspired *On Loving God*, his most popular work.

Catherine of Siena (1347–1380)
Catherine served as a lay member of the Dominican Order and was recognized as a great influence in Italian literature. She and Teresa of Avila were the first women declared a Doctor of the Church, a title recognizing one for making a significant contribution to theology or doctrine through their research, study, or writing. Her most popular work is *The Dialogue of Saint Catherine of Siena*.

Francis of Sales (1567–1622)
The Bishop of Geneva was honored as a Doctor of the Church for his deep faith and writings on spiritual formation. His motto was, "The one who preaches in love, preaches effectively." His *Introduction to the Devout Life* and *Treatise on the Love of God*, rather than being addressed to the clergy—as were most books at the time—were specifically written for laypersons. In his books, he stressed the spiritual reality of a life lived for God.

Francis of Assisi (1181–1226)
Francis was an Italian friar and ordained deacon, as opposed to a monk. Friars took the same vows

of poverty, chastity, and obedience as monks, but served outside of a sequestered monastery. He believed that nature was a reflection of God and called all creatures his "brothers and sisters." His poetry is considered some of finest by secular literary critics. (Unfortunately, the most famous poem attributed to him, "Make Me an Instrument of Thy Peace," was actually written in 1912.) His works were collected in *The Writings of St. Francis of Assisi.*

Jeanne-Marie Bouvier de la Motte Guyon (1648–1717)
At a young age, Madame Guyon was forced into an arranged marriage to a wealthy thirty-eight-year-old. Despite the unhappy marriage, the death of two children, and being imprisoned from 1695 to1703 for her beliefs, she firmly believed in God's perfect plan and that she would be blessed in her suffering. Her works, *A Short and Easy Method of Prayer* and *Spiritual Torrents*, became popular among Protestants in her native France, as well as Italy and Spain and now worldwide.

Ignatius of Loyola (1491–1556)
Ignatius began his career as a Spanish knight, but underwent a spiritual transformation while recovering from serious battle injuries. He abandoned his military career and devoted himself to serving God, studying theology and gaining much from the writings of Francis of Assisi and Thomas à Kempis. In

1539, he founded the Society of Jesus (Jesuits). His most famous writing, *Spiritual Exercises*, was written as a group study for finding God's will in one's life and discerning between good and evil desires.

John of the Cross (1542–1591)
The Spanish friar and priest is best known for his poetry, which is revered both in the church and secular literature. John was encouraged by Teresa of Avila to join her reformation of the Carmelite order in returning it to its strict origins. John was accused of disobedience and sentenced to prison in a monastery where he endured a diet of bread, water, and fish scraps as well as weekly public lashings. While imprisoned, he wrote some of his best-known poetry on paper spirited to him by a guard. After nine months, he escaped and went on to be revered for his books, *Ascent of Mount Carmel* and *The Dark Night of the Soul.* He was later honored as a Doctor of the Church.

Julian of Norwich (1341–1416)
We get this unknown woman's name from her life lived in self-imposed isolation in a tiny room attached to the wall of the Church of St. Julian in Norwich. She was viewed as a spiritual authority, serving as a counselor and advisor, and is now revered by the Anglican and Lutheran churches. Her *Revelations of Divine Love* is believed to be the first book in the English language written by a woman.

Thomas à Kempis (1380–1471)
Thomas Haemmerlein served as a canon regular. Unlike a monk, who limited his ministry within the walls of a monastery, this title describes a religious cleric who lived in community and served in local congregations. He spent his time writing biographies of members of his order as well as copying the Bible by hand at least four times. He also was in charge of instructing young members of his order. In that capacity, he wrote four devotional booklets, which were later combined into one of the world's best-selling books: *The Imitation of Christ.*

Brother Lawrence (1614–1691)
Brother Lawrence of the Resurrection served as a lay brother in a Paris Carmelite monastery, cooking and scrubbing pots and pans. He famously wrote, "For me, the time of business is no different from the time of prayer. In the noise and clatter of my kitchen, while several people are calling for different things at the same time, I experience God in as great tranquility as if I were on my knees in Holy Communion." His book, *The Practice of the Presence of God*, was compiled after his death and is revered by Catholics and Protestants alike, including John Wesley and A.W. Tozer.

Teresa of Avila (1515–1582)
Along with St. John of the Cross, Teresa founded the Discalced (Barefoot) Carmelite order that stressed

modeling the life of Jesus by not owning property, but holding everything in common with other members. Rather than living in isolation, they stressed praying together and working in public ministry. She is considered an important part of Spanish Renaissance literature with her autobiography, *The Life of Teresa of Jesus*, and her most famous and revered work, *The Interior Castle*.

I've arranged the writings of these godly men and women under seven disciplines that I believe lead to intimacy with Christ. (There is no doubt more, but seven seems like a "spiritual" number.)

Community
Discipline
Obedience
Solitude
Meditation
Servanthood
Suffering

The chosen passages are what C.S. Lewis would classify as "mere Christianity" that will be helpful for Catholic, Orthodox, and Protestant believers alike. I've carefully updated these authors' works with modern and inclusive language that remains faithful to the original message. Special thanks to my friend and Catholic lay theologian, Michael Fraley, who compared this Protestant's modernization with the traditional English translations and made valuable suggestions to assure accuracy. I have also included biblical passages that introduce and reinforce the theme of each devotional. Passages taken directly from Scripture have also been attributed.

Most of the works included can be found in early English translations online at the Christian Classic Ethereal Library (http://www.ccel.org).

And so, for this generation, I humbly offer the life-changing messages of these devoted believers who desired to experience true *Intimacy with Christ.*

Introduction

I want to know Christ and experience the mighty power that raised him from the dead.

Philippians 3:10

1. Navigating the Rivers of Life, Part One: *Madame Guyon*
2. Navigating the Rivers of Life, Part Two: *Madame Guyon*

1

Navigating the Rivers of Life, Part One

Madame Guyon

"Anyone who believes in me may come and drink! For the Scriptures declare, 'Rivers of living water will flow from his heart.'"

Jesus, John 7:38

As soon we are drawn to the Son by the Father, and are cleansed by true and sincere confession and repentance, the Spirit creates a desire deep within us to develop an intimate relationship with the Trinity. Our souls feel that we are not created for the amusements and trivial things of the world, but that we have a focus and a purpose that can be found in God alone. This deep desire is a part of our very soul by His design. We sense a loving impatience to purify ourselves and return to our source and origin, as a river leaving its source flows continually toward its goal of the sea.

We can observe that some rivers move slowly while others more rapidly. Some are torrents that rush and rage with frightful impatience and nothing can stop them. They overcome any barrier that tries in vain to slow their course. Any obstruction only doubles their violence as they race to the sea. It's the same way with believers.

Spiritual Torrents, Part 1, Chapter 1

The first class of rivers

The first class of souls are those who, after yielding to Christ, practice some spiritual discipline and acts of charity. Little by little they purify themselves from more obvious sins. They attempt with their little strength to advance—but gradually, weakly, and slowly.

Since their source is not abundant, dryness sometimes causes delay. In times of draught, they dry up altogether. The source is still there, but they don't draw from it so the flow is barely perceptible. These rivers carry little if any merchandise and are dependent on others to meet their needs. They have nothing to offer others, so God seldom uses them. They are like hand pumps which have to be continually primed to yield any water.

O poor and powerless souls! Rather than being like great intellectuals who make prayer a study, our purpose and devotion to Christ must be faithful and pleasing to Him. If we are powerless and incapable of serving Him, we only need to knock at the door and, with humble patience, wait for Him to open the door.

People of great intellect and understanding can't remain silent for a moment before God, so they make a continual Babel before Him. They can teach on any spiritual subject that suggests itself to them. They are well-satisfied with themselves and their devotion. They love to expound upon the preparation and methods for prayer, but they themselves make little progress in their own prayers. After ten or twenty years of their religious exercises, they remain the same.

The second class of rivers

The second class is like large rivers. Flowing with pomp and majesty, their course is slow and steady as they carry heavy cargo. Since their course is direct and easily followed, they go to the sea without mingling with other rivers. Their strength is great, and they are laden with gifts, graces, and godly blessings. They are admired by their peers and shine brighter than the saints of the church.

But they are late in reaching their destination, since they are so serious and slow. There are even some who never reach the sea at all. For the most part, these streams lose themselves in other larger rivers, are lost in back waters, or stopped by levees.

God has designed us to receive His amazing grace. And the staggering amount He gives us should draw us nearer to Him. But second-class believers make use of it for an utterly different end: they rest in it, reflect upon it, look at it, and admire it. They become vain, **complacent**, self-centered, and often destroy their spiritual life. These people are considered admirable—at least to themselves. Sometimes, by a special grace, they are made very helpful to others, particularly if they have been brought from great depths of sin.

This class of people find far greater difficulty in entering the way of faith than the first, since what they already possess is so great and so obviously from God that they will not believe there is anything higher in the church of God. Therefore, they cling to their spiritual status quo.

Spiritual Torrents, Part 1, Chapter 2

2

Navigating the Rivers of Life, Part Two

Madame Guyon

"But those who drink the water I give will never be thirsty again. It becomes a fresh, bubbling spring within them, giving them eternal life."

Jesus, John 4:14

The third class of rivers

What shall we say about the souls in this third way, other than they are torrents of water rushing down the high mountains? They have their source in God Himself and don't have a moment's rest until they are lost in Him. Nothing can stop them! No burdens can be laid upon them! They rush on with a speed that alarms even the most confident sailor. These torrents flow without order, here and there, wherever they can find a passage, having neither regular beds nor an orderly course.

They sometimes become muddy by passing through ground which is not firm, which they wash away with their power. Sometimes they appear to be hopelessly lost, then they reappear for a time, but only to hide again in another crevice, still deeper than the first. It's a sport for these torrents to show themselves, to lose themselves, and to break themselves upon the rocks. Their rapid course is undiscernible. But finally, after many challenges of being dashed against rocks and many times lost and found again, they reach the sea. There, they are lost to never be found.

And there—however poor, humble, useless, or empty of merchandise the torrent may have been—it is wonderfully enriched. For it is not rich with its own abundance, like other rivers, which only bear important cargo or rare treasures. It is rich with the abundance of the sea itself. It now bears on its back the largest vessels. It is actually the sea that supports them, and yet it is the river—having become one with the sea—that bears them. It has not lost its nature, although it is so changed that it no longer can be recognized. It will always remain what it was, yet its identity is lost, not as to reality, but as to quality.

For the river takes on the properties of salt water, which are nothing like it, and the more it loses itself and remains in the sea, the more it exchanges its own nature for that of the sea. For what, then, can't this poor torrent do? Its capacity is unlimited, since it is the same as that of the sea. It is now capable of enriching the whole earth.

O happy loss! Who can set it forth? Who can describe the gain which has been made by this useless and good-for-nothing river, despised and looked upon as a mad thing. Yes, the smallest boat could not trust the river, for it could not restrain itself and would have dragged the tiny vessel with it into the sea.

What can you say about the fate of this torrent, you great rivers? You flow with such majesty. You are the delight and admiration of the world. You glory in the quantity of merchandise carried upon you? And what has become of this poor torrent, which you regarded with contempt or at best with pity? What use can it serve now? The question is what use can it not serve? What does it lack? You are now its servants, since the riches which you possess are only the overflow of its abundance or a fresh supply which you are carrying to it.

The soul, as we have said, proceeds from God. And so, it has a continual pull to return to Him, because He is both its origin and its final end. Its course would be unstoppable if it were not arrested or interrupted by sin and unbelief. Therefore, the heart of man is perpetually in motion, and can find no rest till it returns to its origin and its center, which is God.

Spiritual Torrents, Part 1, Chapter 4

I

Community

"For where two or three gather together as my followers, I am there among them."

Jesus, Matthew 18:20

3

Loving God

Bernard of Clairvaux

Dear friends, let us continue to love one another, for love comes from God. Anyone who loves is a child of God and knows God. But anyone who does not love does not know God, for God is love.

First John 4:7–8

Why should God be loved so much?

First, He deserves our love. Could there be any greater reason than this: He gave Himself for us when we were unworthy of His love? And being God, what better gift could He offer than Himself? So, if we want to know why God wants our love in return, here is the greatest reason: "Because he loved us first" (4:19).

Second, because He has loved us so much. The apostle John explains, "For this is how God loved the world: He gave his one and only Son, so that everyone who believes in him will not perish but have eternal life" (John 3:16). The apostle Paul adds, "Since he did not spare even his own Son but gave him up for us all . . ." (Rom. 8:32). And Jesus Himself says, "'There is no greater love than to lay down one's life for one's friends'" (John 15:13). This is His wonderful love that does not seek its own way (see 1 Cor. 13:5).

Paul writes, "For since our friendship with God was restored by the death of his Son while we were still his enemies, we will certainly be saved through the life of his Son" (Rom. 5:10). So, it was God who freely loved us; even loving while we were yet so unloving! And how great was this love of His.

This is the claim which God—the holy, the supreme, and all-powerful One—has placed upon each of us who are corrupted, earthly-minded, and weak: to love Him. And God's wondrous love for sinful people empowers them to overcome sin and live a life of His love.

On Loving God, Chapter 1

4

Loving Ourselves and Others

Julian of Norwich

When we were utterly helpless, Christ came at just the right time and died for us sinners. Now, most people would not be willing to die for an upright person, though someone might perhaps be willing to die for a person who is especially good. But God showed his great love for us by sending Christ to die for us while we were still sinners.

Romans 5:6–8

This is the powerful love of our gracious Lord: He cares for us so tenderly while we are still in rebellion to His plan for us. He knows us intimately and reveals our sins to us in the sweet light of mercy and grace. When we see our true self so foul—with our intense displeasure of Him expressed in our selfish thoughts and actions—we are stirred by the Holy Spirit to come to Him in repentance, in prayer, and with the desire to make amends to avoid the wrath of God. Then we find a rest in our soul, a softness in our conscience, and finally a hope that God has truly forgiven our sins.

Then our gracious Lord Himself brings joy and gladness to our souls as He welcomes us into His family. It is as though we have been released from pain and prison! He sweetly says, "My beloved child, I am glad you came to Me. In all your sorrow, I have always been with you. Now we are one in love." In our worship of God, we receive joy as if we were now present in heaven itself. This is the gracious passion of Christ and the working of the Holy Spirit.

Please understand this truth: by the great goodness of God, all essential needs will be provided, and we will enjoy His peace and love since we are truly saved. But because we may not have this fullness of peace and love here, we must all the more seek sweet prayer and a loving desire for our Lord Jesus. For He always longs to bring us the fullness of Himself as we spiritually thirst for Him.

But be careful with all this spiritual comfort! May we never be so foolish as to say, "If it is true that I am unconditionally loved, then it is good to sin so we may receive more grace." Beware of this thinking! It is the enemy of true love. We must hate sin because of love! For if all the possible pains of this life and death were laid upon us, we would rather choose all that suffering rather than sin, for it is so vile and so greatly to be hated. There is no harder hell than sin, for a righteous soul has no hell but sin.

We intensely long for love and meekness, for by the working of mercy and grace we are made entirely lovely and pure. God the Father and God the Son are willing, mighty, and wise to save us. For the Son obeyed all the laws of God and taught us to do good against all opposition. Here, may we see that He Himself is love, and He teaches us to love as He loves. For He desires that we be like Him in the wholeness of endless love for ourselves and others.

Because He loved us and was broken for our sins, we should not be broken for our sins by judging ourselves. We should forever hate sin and endlessly love ourselves as God loves us. And in His Word is endless comfort: "The LORD keeps you from all harm and watches over your life" (Ps. 121:7).

Revelation of Divine Love, 13th Revelation, Chapter 40

5

Loving God Because He Is God

Bernard of Clairvaux

This is real love—not that we loved God, but that he loved us and sent his Son as a sacrifice to take away our sins.

First John 4:10

So, in the beginning we love God; not for God's sake, but for our own. We know how little we can do by ourselves and how much we could do with God's help. If we will only align ourselves with God, we will learn of His sure support.

But when troubles and heartaches occur again and again, we turn to God for unfailing help. Even a heart as hard as iron and cold as marble can be softened by unselfishly loving God, simply because He is God. So, let frequent troubles drive us to frequent prayer. Then, surely, we will personally see how gracious the Lord is (see Ps. 34:8).

Therefore, once we realize His goodness, it draws us to love Him unselfishly, even more than our own needs compel us. As the Samaritans told the woman who announced that it was Christ who was at the well, "Then they said to the woman, 'Now we believe, not just because of what you told us, but because we have heard him ourselves. Now we know that he is indeed the Savior of the world'" (John 4:42). In the same way in our human nature, we say, "No longer do we love God because of our necessity, but because we have tasted and seen how gracious the Lord is."

Our physical needs have their own way of talking, proclaiming benefits they have received from God's favor. Once we recognize this, it won't be hard to fulfill the commandment to love our neighbors. For if we truly love God, we will truly love all His creatures. Such love is pure and doesn't find it a burden to obey His command to purify our souls and obey the Spirit in showing "sincere love to each other as brothers and sisters" (1 Pet. 1:22). If we love as we should, we'll consider this command as simply just. Such love is praiseworthy, since it is spontaneous and pure. So, "let's not merely say that we love each other; let us show the truth by our actions" (1 John 3:18). We love in this way, even as we are loved. We don't seek our own desires, but those of Christ, even as He didn't seek His own welfare but ours!

This was the psalmist's love when He sang, "Give thanks to the Lord, for he is good! His faithful love endures forever" (Ps. 118:1). Whoever praises God for His essential goodness, and not merely because of the benefits He has poured out, truly loves God for God's sake rather than one's own. The psalmist was not speaking of such love when he warns of those who "consider themselves fortunate and are applauded for their success" (Ps. 49:18). No, this is a higher love we have: to love God solely because He is God.

On Loving God, Chapter 9

6

Preparing for Intimacy with Christ

John of the Cross

But to all who believed him and accepted him, he gave the right to become children of God.

John 1:12

God reveals Himself most fully to souls who have progressed furthest in love; to the one who conforms most completely to His will. That soul is completely united and spiritually transformed in God.

However, as I explained, the more tightly a soul is wrapped around created things and its own abilities—by desires and habits—the less prepared it is for intimacy with Christ. It's not given God full opportunity to transform it supernaturally. We need only to strip ourselves of earthly things that are unlike and contrary to God. God communicates naturally through created things, but He desires to communicate supernaturally by His grace.

God Himself gives us the power to become His children—that is, to be transformed by Him. He doesn't give this to those born of blood or of natural character or temperament. Neither by the will of the flesh, that is of the free will of human strength and ability. And still less by human will such as thinking, judging, and understanding.

He gives power to none of these to become children of God, but only to those that are born of God. When we are being born again through grace and dying to everything that is of our old nature, we are raised above ourselves and receive from God this rebirth and adoption, which transcends all that can be imagined.

It is clear then that the preparation of our souls for this intimacy with Christ is not something we perceive, feel, or imagine. But it's our purity through Him and His love that brings perfect commitment to God and detachment from everything that is not of Him.

Ascent of Mount Carmel, Book 2, Chapter 5

7

Becoming Intimate with Christ

Teresa of Avila

Jesus replied, "'You must love the LORD your God with all your heart, all your soul, and all your mind.' This is the first and greatest commandment. A second is equally important: 'Love your neighbor as yourself.'"

Matthew 22:37–39

What do you think, my friends, is Christ's desire for us? To be made perfect in heart (see 5:48) and be made one with His Father as He prayed we might. So, what must we do to obtain this? I confess it is very painful for me to write on this subject, for I see that through my own fault, I am so far from obtaining this perfection. There is no need for us to receive special favors from God to become conformed to His will. He has done enough in giving us His Son to teach the way.

Our Lord asks only two things of us: love for Him and for our neighbor. This love is what we must strive to obtain. If we practice these virtues perfectly, we will be fulfilling His purpose and doing His will: to be united with Him.

But, as I wrote, we are very far from obeying and serving our great Master perfectly in these two matters. May His majesty give us the grace to receive union with Him. His power is ours if we desire it. I think the most certain sign that we're keeping these two commandments is that we have a genuine love for others. We can't know if we truly love God—there are strong reasons to think so—but there can be no doubt about whether we love neighbor or not.

We must be sure that, in proportion to how we are growing in our love for our brothers and sisters, we are increasing in our love for God. Christ our King has such a tender love for us that I know He will repay our love for others by increasing in a thousand different ways our love for Him. We must watch very carefully that we may be faultless in this love (see Eph. 1:4). I believe that human nature is so evil that we can't show love for our neighbor unless it is rooted in the love of God.

We might know ourselves well enough to realize that we've not yet attained this perfect intimacy with Christ. However, when we feel devotion, sweetness, or become lost in quiet contemplation, we can almost think we have. But believe me, we have not yet obtained it if we don't have love for our neighbor. Beg our Lord to grant you His perfect love and leave the rest to Him.

The Interior Castle, The Fifth Mansions, Chapter 3

8

Being Known by Our Love

Ignatius of Loyola

Jesus replied, "All who love me will do what I say. My Father will love them, and we will come and make our home with each of them."

John 14:23

We must be careful to preserve a pure heart in our love for God. We should love nothing but Him and desire to converse with no one but Him. In talking with our neighbor, may it be for the love of God and not for our own pleasure and delight. We should speak what is necessary and for the building up of ourselves and others. Avoid topics that don't profit the soul, such as novel and worldly affairs. We should always talk about those things that produce humility and unselfishness, rather than laughter or complaining. Don't try to impress others with wit, eloquence, or elegance, but model Christ, who didn't desire these things, but chose to be humbled or despised rather than honored and respected.

We shouldn't wish to see or do anything that couldn't be done in the presence of God and His creatures, for we are always in His presence. We shouldn't stubbornly argue with anyone, but rather patiently give our reasoning for the truth so our neighbor won't remain in error. We should, however, never claim the upper hand.

One of the things we must be very firm about if we're to please our Lord, is to cast far away anything that could alienate us from the love of our brothers and sisters. We should make every effort to love them with kindhearted love, for Christ has said, "Your love for one another will prove to the world that you are my disciples" (John 13:35).

If we do anything that doesn't build up the body in love, we shouldn't be looked down upon or become discouraged and want to give up. Let us humble ourselves and ask forgiveness from those who might have been harmed by our bad example. We should thank God, who has permitted us to be humbled, so that we can be known by all for what we are. We shouldn't want to appear better in the eyes of people than we are in the eyes of God. As fellow believers, we should remember that any of us can fall into even greater weakness and should ask God to strengthen us as well as them.

As the apostle Paul writes, "Let everyone see that you are considerate in all you do" (Phil. 4:5). We should never postpone a good work, no matter how small it may be, with the thought of doing something greater later. It's a very common temptation of the Enemy to always be looking to the perfection of the future with little value in the present. Let us all persevere in the work to which God calls us and make it our first priority. Don't be gazing at things far off that are preventing us from taking advantage of opportunities to serve near at hand.

A Letter to Brother Joseph

9

"Loving as I Have Loved You"

Francis of Sales

"So now I am giving you a new commandment: Love each other. Just as I have loved you, you should love each other. Your love for one another will prove to the world that you are my disciples."

Jesus, John 13:34–35

Do you, my children, love everyone with the pure love of Christ? Do you have deep relationships with those who are good and true? The purer the bond which unites us, the much richer our friendships will be. If our relationship is based on knowledge, it is praiseworthy, but it's even better if based on love, devotion, and Christian completeness. God knows how very precious that friendship is! Precious because it comes from God and it desires Him. God is the link that binds us together and it will last forever in Him.

Truly it is a blessed thing to love on earth as we hope to love in heaven, beginning a relationship here which will endure forever there. I'm not speaking of simple charity—a love due to all humankind—but a spiritual friendship which binds our souls together, leading us to share devotions and spiritual interests. We must have one mind between us, so we can rejoice, "How wonderful and pleasant it is when [we] live together in harmony!" (Ps. 133:1). Our common devotion—which flows from one heart to the other—makes for us a friendship in which the Lord promises His blessing and life forevermore.

To my mind, all other friendships are but a shadow in this respect. The links between believers are a steel bond of true devotion compared to the fragile glass of worldly friendships.

There are some who will tell us that we should avoid special friendships as they may obsess our hearts, distract our minds, create jealousy, and so on. Some saintly and devout writers argue that individual friendships and deep relationships are a great hinderance to our spiritual life. But they are confusing things. This is not the case!

No one can deny that our dear Lord loved John, Lazarus, Martha, and Mary with a special, tender friendship since we are told so in the holy Scripture. And we know that Paul dearly loved Mark.

Gregory Nazianzus, the archbishop of Constantinople, always boasted of His friendship with Bishop Basil of Caesarea. He writes: "It seemed as though we had two bodies, we had only one soul. We can affirm that we were two in one and one in two—our only goal being to grow in holiness and to mold our present lives to our future hopes, and so reject this mortal world before our death."

So we see that the highest grace does not lie in being without friendships, but in having only those that are good, holy, and true.

Introduction to the Devout Life, Part 3, Chapter 19

10

Fleeing Poisonous Relationships

Francis of Sales

Run from anything that stimulates youthful lusts. Instead, pursue righteous living, faithfulness, love, and peace. Enjoy the companionship of those who call on the Lord with pure hearts.

Second Timothy 2:22

Beware, my children: the sap of the giant hogweed plant looks just like wholesome honey, but is extremely poisonous. It's dangerous to mistake one for the other, or to mix them, hoping the goodness of the one will counteract the harmful effects of the other.

In the same way, we must be on our guard to not be deceived when making friendships, especially between persons of the opposite sex, as Satan often deludes those who love each other. They may begin with virtuous affection, but if discretion is lacking, familiarity will creep in, and then sensuality, until their love becomes physical.

Even in spiritual love, there is a danger if we're not careful! However, the purity and transparency of spiritual affections show Satan's stains more promptly. Consequently, when he seeks to intervene, he does it stealthily and almost imperceptibly. We can distinguish between worldly friendship and that which is good and holy, just as one can discern the poisonous honey from the wholesome.

Poisonous honey tastes sweeter than the ordinary—and so worldly friendships are filled with sweet and enticing words, compliments on appearance, and sensual conversation. That strange honey of false friendship causes lightheadedness and disturbing thoughts; it makes its victim stumble in the ways of purity and devotion. It displays itself in sensual looks and caresses, emotional excesses, petty complaints of not being loved, slight but questionable familiarities, embraces, and so on, which are sure foretastes of evil.

True friendship has its foundation in Christ, speaks a simple and honest language, and boasts of nothing but the grace of God.

Lastly, this poisonous honey leaves an extremely bitter taste behind. False friendships turn to evil desires, compromises, slander, deceit, sorrow, confusion, and jealousy. Too often it ends in overt sin. But pure friendships are always the same: modest, courteous, and loving. They do not change except for an increasingly pure and perfect union—the kind blessed in heaven.

Introduction to the Devout Life, Part 3, Chapter 10

11

Keep Ourselves United in the Spirit

Ignatius of Loyola

Always be humble and gentle. Be patient with each other, making allowance for each other's faults because of your love. Make every effort to keep yourselves united in the Spirit, binding yourselves together with peace. For there is one body and one Spirit, just as you have been called to one glorious hope for the future.

Ephesians 4:2–4

Instructions for speaking at a public meeting

In all our conversations, we should be slow to speak and say little. Be ready to listen for long periods of time until each one has had his or her say. We should answer the questions put to us—and stop. If a response is required, may our replies be as brief as possible.

In dealing with people of position or influence—whom we hope to make an impact for the greater glory of God our Lord—let's first consider their personalities and temperaments and then adapt ourselves to them.

- If they are animated, quick, and cheerful in speech, follow their lead while speaking to them of good and holy things. Don't be serious, glum, and reserved.
- If they seem shy, withdrawn, slow in speech, serious and weighty in their words, use the same manner with them, because such a demeanor will be pleasing to them.
- If we are dealing with someone of a slower temperament, we create trouble if we speak too quickly.

Follow the apostle Paul's example as he writes, "I try to find common ground with everyone" (1 Cor. 9:22).

Keep in mind we all have different personalities, and we may be in danger of not coming to an agreement, since we may not be of the same mind. If someone is speaking from the heart, reply from the heart. If someone is speaking on an intellectual level, respond on an intellectual level. We should study closely the opinions of those who are speaking, and be determined to be patient and not get annoyed with them, especially if we know they are in poor health.

Whenever we wish to win people over and engage them in the greater service of God our Lord, we should use the same strategy for good that the Enemy employs to draw a good soul to evil. The Enemy gains entrance into the person, not by opposing his ways but by praising them. He is agreeable with the soul, suggesting good and holy thoughts that bring peace to the good soul. But little by little, he shifts to his point of view, always portraying some error or illusion under the appearance of something good, but which will always be evil.

So, we may lead others to good by agreeing with them on a certain good point, leaving aside whatever we may disagree upon. By gaining their confidence, we'll have better success. In this sense, we enter their world with them, then introduce them to our world.

Be kind and compassionate with those who are sad or tempted; speak patiently with them. Show great joy and cheerfulness, both inward and outward. Guide them to the opposite of what they feel, for their greater benefit and comfort. In everything we say—especially when we are trying to restore peace and are giving spiritual advice—we must be on our guard. And remember that everything we say may or will become public.

From letter sent to Paschase Broët and Alfonso Salmerón

12

Speaking the Truth in Love

Ignatius of Loyola

We will speak the truth in love, growing in every way more and more like Christ, who is the head of his body, the church. He makes the whole body fit together perfectly. As each part does its own special work, it helps the other parts grow, so that the whole body is healthy and growing and full of love.

Ephesians 4:15–16

Be slow to speak at meetings. Be considerate and kind, especially when it comes to decisions on matters under discussion.

First listen quietly, so that you may understand the meaning, intentions, and wishes of those who do speak. Then we will better know when to speak and when to be silent. When these or other matters are under discussion, we should consider the argument on both sides without showing any preference for our own opinion. Avoid bringing division to the group.

We should not quote anyone in the meeting as supporting our opinion—especially if they are someone of importance—unless this has been thoroughly arranged beforehand. And I would deal with everyone on an equal basis, never taking sides with anyone.

If the matters being discussed are something of which we cannot or should not be silent, then we should give our opinion with the greatest possible humility and sincerity. And always end with the words "with due respect for a better opinion."

Letter to those attending the Council of Trent, 1545

II

Discipline

I don't mean to say that I have already achieved these things or that I have already reached perfection. But I press on to possess that perfection for which Christ Jesus first possessed me. No, dear brothers and sisters, I have not achieved it, but I focus on this one thing: Forgetting the past and looking forward to what lies ahead, I press on to reach the end of the race and receive the heavenly prize for which God, through Christ Jesus, is calling us.

Philippians 3:12–14

13

Committing All Our Desires to Christ

Thomas à Kempis

Work hard so you can present yourself to God and receive his approval. Be a good worker, one who does not need to be ashamed and who correctly explains the word of truth.

Second Timothy 2:15

The Christ
My child, you still have many things to learn, which you have not yet learned well.

The Disciple
What are they, Lord?

The Christ
To commit all your desires to My good pleasure and not to be a lover of yourself. Your desires often excite you and propel you forward, but ask yourself if these actions are for your own benefit or for My honor. If it is Me that you seek, then you will be content with whatever I plan for you. But if any of these pursuits are your own initiative, be aware that they will hinder you and weigh you down.

So beware of acting on something you have planned, without taking counsel from Me. You may find that what you thought as very good and would please you, has now caused regret and displeasure. Not every pleasant desire which seems good should be followed; neither should any unpleasant thing be immediately avoided. Sometimes, it is beneficial to use restraint even in good desires and wishes. You may become distracted with it, or your lack of discipline may become a stumbling block to others, or perhaps opposition may suddenly disturb you and bring confusion.

Sometimes, indeed, it is necessary to use strong self-discipline to strive against sensual appetites. Don't consider what your human nature wants or doesn't want, but strive to become subject—willingly or unwillingly—to My Spirit. Sometimes you may feel enslaved by your desires and struggle to be ready for full surrender to My good purpose for you. But you will learn to be content with little, to be delighted with simple things, and never to complain about any inconvenience.

The Imitation of Christ, Book 3, Chapter 15

14

Making Sensuality an Obedient Servant

Author of The Cloud of Unknowing

Because we belong to the day, we must live decent lives for all to see. Don't participate in the darkness of wild parties and drunkenness, or in sexual promiscuity and immoral living, or in quarreling and jealousy.

Romans 13:13

Sensuality is the power of soul that guides and controls our physical senses of the world around us. It detects what is pleasing and what is not. One part gives attention to the needs of the body and the other to the lusts of the physical senses.

This power alerts the body when any of its needs are lacking, but it also stirs up more than is physically necessary, such as lusts of the flesh. It complains at the lack of pleasant sensations and is highly delighted in experiencing them. Both its passions and actions are controlled by the mind.

Before Adam and Eve sinned, sensuality was such an obedient servant to the will that it never desired any improper pleasure or complaint. There was no spiritual expression of liking or disliking wrought by the devil in the physical senses. But that is no longer the case.

Now, unless sensuality is governed by the will by God's grace, it will not tolerate meekness or moderation. Our sinful nature wants to avoid any discomforts and become unrestrained in lustful pleasures. It willingly and shamelessly wallows in the mud of the world as a pig. In its foul flesh it becomes more animal and carnal than human or spiritual.

So, my spiritual friend, as you see, we have fallen into such wretchedness because of sin. If we do not understand how blindly and easily we can be deceived in our understanding of this working, we will fall.

Whenever our minds are occupied with any physical thing—no matter how good the purpose may be—we are beneath the purpose of our lives.

The Cloud of Unknowing, Chapter 66

15

Being Crucified with Christ

Teresa of Avila

My old self has been crucified with Christ. It is no longer I who live, but Christ lives in me. So I live in this earthly body by trusting in the Son of God, who loved me and gave himself for me.

Galatians 2:20

Die! Die as the silkworm dies when it has fulfilled the purpose of its creation. Then we will see God and be immersed in His greatness, as the little silkworm is enveloped in its cocoon.

Now, let's see what becomes of the silkworm. Like it, our souls have become entirely dead to the world, and only then do we burst forth like a lovely little white butterfly!

Oh, how great God is! How beautiful is the soul after having been immersed in God's grandeur and united closely to Him for but a short time!

Truly, we don't recognize our new selves: a white butterfly so different compared to what we were as a repulsive caterpillar. We realize that we don't deserve so great a transformation and the grace which brought it about. Our souls desire to praise our Lord

God, and we are willing to sacrifice ourselves and die a thousand deaths for Him. We want all people to know God even while we are bitterly grieved by how they now offend Him.

After our souls have received these favors, we strive to make further progress and experience great things. Oh, to see the restlessness of this charming little butterfly, although never in its life has it been more tranquil and at peace! May God be praised! We don't know where to light or take rest. Everything on earth disgusts us after we have experienced this new life. God has given us new nectar which leaves fresh graces behind it at every sip. We despise the life we led while yet a caterpillar, slowly weaving our cocoon strand by strand.

Now that our wings have grown and we can fly, how could it be content to crawl? All that we can do for God seems nothing compared to our soul's desire. We no longer wonder why the saints chose to suffer for Him. We now know by experience how our Lord aids and transforms our soul until we no longer seem to be the same in appearance and character.

Once we feared godly discipline, but now we have strong courage to avoid ungodly relationships and earthly possessions. We now separate from what we once loved and increase our love for godly things. Even if God's rightful claims seem a burden, we fear contact with worldly things so we won't offend Him.

We weary of things which once gave pleasure, realizing that no true rest can be found in earthly things. No wonder this beautiful butterfly, estranged from earthly things, seeks peace elsewhere. Where can the poor little creature go? It cannot return from where it came from, for it now depends upon God's pleasure.

However, after experiencing such amazing grace, fresh trials will begin to afflict the mind! In fact, in one way or another, we must carry the cross all our lives. If someone tells me that since attaining intimacy with Christ, they have enjoyed constant peace and consolation, I would reply that they could never have reached that state. Their spiritual satisfaction is based on emotion alone. It might even be a false sweetness caused by the devil, who gives peace for a time only to wage far fiercer war later on. I do not mean that those who reach this stage of union with Christ possess no peace; they do so in a very high degree. However, their sorrows, though extremely severe, provide spiritual benefits from so good a Source as to produce both peace and happiness.

The Interior Castle, The Fifth Mansions, Chapter 2

16

Giving Up Our Own Way

John of the Cross

Dear brothers and sisters, I plead with you to give your bodies to God because of all he has done for you. Let them be a living and holy sacrifice—the kind he will find acceptable. This is truly the way to worship him. Don't copy the behavior and customs of this world, but let God transform you into a new person by changing the way you think. Then you will learn to know God's will for you, which is good and pleasing and perfect.

Romans 12:1–2

Oh, that we could understand, practice, and experience what our Savior taught us concerning self-denial! How different it is from what so many think is proper for spiritual persons upon the road to heaven. They are content to practice virtues, continue in prayer, and talk about dying to self, but they become resistant to taking up their cross. They avoid separation from the world, displayed in godly love, selflessness, and spiritual purity for which the Lord commends us. But they replace feeding and clothing their natural selves with spiritual feelings and comforts, rather than stripping themselves of all things for God's sake. For they think it's sufficient to deny themselves worldly things without denying and purifying themselves from even spiritual comforts.

So, when confronted with solid and perfect spirituality, which is not all sweetness in God, they flee from it like death itself. These dry, distasteful trials are the true spiritual cross. Those who seek only sweetness and delectable communion with God are not practicing self-denial and detachment of spirit, but spiritual gluttony. So, they become enemies of the cross of Christ.

True spirituality seeks for God's sake that which is distasteful rather than that which is delectable. It inclines itself to suffering rather than to comfort. It desires to go without all blessings for God's sake so it can possess God Himself. It endures spiritual dryness and earthly afflictions rather than to enjoy sweet communications, knowing that this is to follow Christ and to deny oneself. As He teaches, "If any of you wants to be my follower, you must give up your own way, take up your cross, and follow me. If you try to hang on to your life, you will lose it. But if you give up your life for my sake and for the sake of the Good News, you will save it" (Mark 8:34–35).

If you are seeking God's favors and benefits, you are seeking yourself. But to seek God Himself and to choose for His sake what is distasteful to the world, this is the love of God.

Ascent of Mount Carmel, Book 2, Chapter 7

17

Loving Ourselves Only in Christ

Bernard of Clairvaux

"If you refuse to take up your cross and follow me, you are not worthy of being mine. If you cling to your life, you will lose it; but if you give up your life for me, you will find it."

Jesus, Matthew 10:38–39

How blessed are those who reach the point of loving themselves only in God. The righteous stand like strong mountains, O God. Such love as this is God's hill on which He is pleased to dwell, as Scripture teaches:

> Who may climb the mountain of the Lord?
> Who may stand in his holy place? (Ps. 24:3)
>
> Oh, that I had wings like a dove;
> then I would fly away and rest! (55:6)
>
> Jerusalem is where he lives;
> Mount Zion is his home. (76:2)

How I suffer far from Jerusalem. It pains me to live in a distant land (see 120:5). When will this flesh and blood, this earthen vessel (see 2 Cor. 4:7) which is my soul's temple, fly off to the mountain? When will my soul, so captivated by divine love that it forgets itself as it longs wholly for God, be joined and be one spirit with Him? "My health may fail, and my spirit may grow weak, / but God remains the strength of my heart; / he is mine forever" (Ps. 73:26).

We count ourselves blessed and holy to be granted this heavenly love in this earthly life! It is indeed heavenly, for even an instant, to lose oneself, to be emptied, and swallowed up in God's love. If for a rapturous moment we humans feel that heavenly joy, we are to be envied.

Our daily struggles, our frail bodies, our physical needs, the corruption around us, and the lack of brotherly love draws us to the God of love. These things cause us to call for God to reenter our lives. We cry out, "'I am in trouble, Lord. Help me!'" (Isa. 38:14). "Oh, what a miserable person I am! Who will free me from this life that is dominated by sin and death?" (Rom. 7:24).

Since the prophet writes, "All who claim me as their God . . . I have made them for my glory" (Isa. 43:7), surely we must conform ourselves, as much as we can, to His will. All our loves and affections should center on Him. In all things we should seek only to do His will—not to please ourselves. And real happiness will come, not in gratifying our desires or in gaining temporary pleasures, but in accomplishing God's will for us. So let us pray every day: "'May your will be done on earth, as it is in heaven'" (Matt. 6:10).

On Loving God, Chapter 10

18

Losing Ourselves in Christ

Bernard of Clairvaux

"'You must love the Lord *your God with all your heart, all your soul, all your strength, and all your mind.' And, 'Love your neighbor as yourself.'"*

Jesus, Luke 10:27

O pure and holy love! O sweet and gracious affection! O pure and cleansed purpose, thoroughly washed and purged from any impurity of selfishness, and sweetened in union with the divine will! To reach this state is to become godlike.

It is like a drop of water poured into wine; it loses itself, and takes on the color and flavor of wine. Or as a bar of iron, heated red-hot, becomes like fire itself, forgetting its own nature. Or as the air, radiant with sunbeams, seems not so much to be illuminated as to be light itself. So, through the power of Christ, our human affections can melt away by a miraculous transformation into the will of God.

For how could God be all in all, if anything merely human remained in humans? While we may remain in human flesh, our spirit can reflect another beauty, a higher power, a greater glory. When will that be?

I thirst for God, the living God.
When can I go and stand before him?
(Ps. 42:2)

My heart has heard you say,
"Come and talk with me."
And my heart responds,
"Lord, I am coming." (Ps. 27:8)

I will meet You in Your Temple, which is now our bodies and Your church.

In this life, I don't think we can fully and perfectly obey the command, "'You must love the Lord your God with all your heart, all your soul, all your strength, and all your mind.' And, 'Love your neighbor as yourself'" (Luke 10:27). For in this life, the soul must think about and care for the body and the mind must guard itself from trouble, and by God's grace develop physically and spiritually. So, it is impossible to offer up all ourselves to God, to completely desire His face, so long as we must fulfill our purposes and desires to these fragile, weak bodies of ours.

While we cannot obtain perfect, peaceful, and spiritually submissive love while in these mortal bodies, we can obtain a degree of it—not by human effort, but by God's power to provide it. Then the soul will easily reach that highest stage, because no lusts of the flesh will slow its eager entrance into the joy of its Lord and no troubles will disturb its peace.

Certainly, the holy martyrs enjoyed this grace, in some degree at least, before they laid down their victorious bodies? Surely it was immeasurable strength of love which empowered their souls, enabling them to laugh at bodily torments and to yield their lives gladly to death.

On Loving God, Chapter 10

19

Serving Christ Out of Only Love

Catherine of Siena

We prove ourselves by our purity, our understanding, our patience, our kindness, by the Holy Spirit within us, and by our sincere love.

Second Corinthians 6:6

The Father

Some of My followers have become trustworthy servants, serving Me faithfully, not with a cowering fear of punishment, but rather with love. However, this love is imperfect if they serve Me with a view to their own profit, delight, and pleasure which they find in Me.

Do you know what proves the imperfection of this love? When I withdraw the comfort they find in Me, in a short time their love for their neighbor grows weak and insufficient and often disappears. And if I withdraw from their mind in order to exercise them in virtue and raise them above imperfection and allow them to fall into battles and perplexities, their love for Me grows weak. I do this so, coming to perfect self-knowledge, they will realize that of themselves, they are nothing and have no grace. In this time of battle, they will fly to Me for their sole support, seeking Me alone with true humility. I treat them this way by taking away My comfort, but not My grace.

During this time, those without strong commitment to Me, will relax their energy and turn back, and sometimes justify themselves by saying, "I'm not seeing any benefit in my faith." They do all this because they feel deprived of mental satisfaction. Such souls act imperfectly, because they are still wrapped up in spiritual self-love. If they would free themselves from this self-centeredness, they would truly see that everything proceeds from Me. I created them and empowered them to live a holy life. My disciples should see and know that I wish only their good through the blood of My only Son, in whose blood they are cleansed from all wickedness and enabled to know My truth. We created humans in Our image and likeness and recreated them with the blood of My Son, making them children of adoption.

Imperfect disciples use Me only for their own profit and relax their love for their neighbor. First, they come to nothing through the fear of pain. Then they slacken their spiritual pace. And if they see that good deeds and comfort are not returned back to them, they cease to serve their neighbor. This happens because their original love was impure, for they gave their neighbor the same imperfect love that they gave to Me. It is a love based only on their desire for their own benefit. If they do not recognize this imperfection, they will turn back.

The Dialogue of Saint Catherine of Siena

20

Being United in Christ

Catherine of Siena

May you experience the love of Christ, though it is too great to understand fully. Then you will be made complete with all the fullness of life and power that comes from God.

Ephesians 3:19

The Father

For those who desire eternal life, a pure, deep-down love is necessary. It is not enough to flee sins for fear of punishment or to embrace virtue for your own advantage. Sin should be abandoned because it is displeasing to Me, and virtue should be loved for My sake.

It is true that, generally speaking, every person is first called in this way, but this is because the soul is imperfect at first. But you must advance from imperfection to perfection. Your soul should be alive with a generous love for Me, with a pure and virtuous heart that takes no thought for itself.

It was with this imperfect love that the apostle Peter loved the likeable and good Jesus, with whom he enjoyed a pleasant relationship. But when the time of trouble came, he failed so disgracefully. He could not bear any pain himself, so his terror of the very approach of pain caused him to fall, and deny My Son with the words, "I do not know him!"

The soul who comes to Me with servant-like fear or mercenary love alone, falls into many troubles. Such souls should arise and become brothers and sisters, serve Me without regard for themselves or for any rewards they will acquire. Yes, I am the Rewarder of every labor and render to all people according to their labor. If these souls do not abandon the exercise of holy prayer and their other good works, but go on with perseverance to increase their virtues, they will arrive at the state of family love, because I respond to them with the same love with which they love Me.

So, if they love Me as a servant loves his master, I pay them their wages according to what they deserve, but I do not reveal myself to them. Secrets are only revealed to a dear friend, who has become one with his friend and not to a servant. But if they remain in this state of mercenary love, I will not open myself to them.

However, it is true that a servant may so advance by virtuous love that he or she becomes a very dear friend. And I will reveal Myself to them, as My Truth said in these words: "Those who accept my commandments and obey them are the ones who love me. And because they love me, my Father will love them. And I will love them and reveal myself to each of them" (John 14:21).

This is the state of two dear friends, for though they are two in body, yet they are one in soul through the affection of love, because love transforms the lover into the object loved, and where two friends have one soul, there can be no secret between them. My Son and I "will come and make our home with each of them" (John 14:23).

The Dialogue of Saint Catherine of Siena

21

Desiring Nothing That God Doesn't Desire

Author of The Cloud of Unknowing

Fix your thoughts on what is true, and honorable, and right, and pure, and lovely, and admirable. Think about things that are excellent and worthy of praise.

Philippians 4:8

We must take care that we don't think or desire anything apart from what God desires of us. Everything we know and feel should be submitted to the will of God so that all else is forgotten. Understand that in this spiritual work, we are not only to forget all others' deeds but our own as well. For this is the sign of perfect love for God, to not only love what He loves more than ourselves, but to hate anything we love more than Him.

This is what we are to do with ourselves. We should hate and be impatient with anything in our mind that is not of God. And no wonder you hate to think of yourself when you have sinned. There is a foul, stinking obstruction between you and God. That obstruction is none other than yourself.

But after we have repented and been forgiven of our sins, we put memories and feeling about ourselves and others behind us. Our attitudes and feelings toward others now depends on us. If we actively choose to forget our own and others' past, there will be a pure awareness and feeling of ourselves in God's work in us. This allows us to experience and continue to work in being perfected through God.

The Cloud of Unknowing, Chapter 43

22

Keeping Our Minds on Christ

Brother Lawrence

"Seek the Kingdom of God above all else, and live righteously, and he will give you everything you need."

Jesus, Matthew 6:33

I have found many books teaching different methods of going to God and various practices of the spiritual life. I feared this study would confuse me rather than gain what I sought after: nothing but to become wholly God's.

I resolved to give my all to the All. So, after giving myself wholly to God and obtaining forgiveness of my sin, I renounced everything that was not Him. I began to live as if there was no one and nothing but Him and me in the world.

Sometimes I viewed myself as a poor criminal before the feet of a judge. Other times, I imagined Him in my heart as my Father. Often, I worshipped Him continuously, keeping in mind His holy presence.

Other times, I wandered from Him. I felt great pain in this, but I continued in my spiritual disciplines despite the difficulties. I felt troubled and conflicted when my thoughts involuntarily wandered.

So I made it my business to meditate on God all day long with formal times of prayer as well as continual prayer every hour and minute. I found this easy, even when I was busy with my work. I drove from my mind every thought that could interrupt my thoughts of God.

This has been my common practice since I entered the ministry. And even though I have not done it perfectly, still I have found great benefits in it. I know very well that I've been able to do this only through the mercy and goodness of God, because we can do nothing without Him. But when we are faithful to keep ourselves in His holy presence, and meditate on Him always, this keeps us from offending Him and willfully doing anything that may displease Him. It also grants us a holy freedom so we can speak freely with God and have our needs met by His grace. As we repeat this discipline of consciously meditating on Him, it becomes natural to us.

Give Him thanks with me for the great goodness He shows to us. I can't praise Him enough for the many favors He has granted a miserable sinner like me. May all things praise Him. Amen.

Practicing the Presence of God, First Letter

23

Loving Christ More Than His Gifts

Thomas à Kempis

Jesus asked Simon Peter, "Simon son of John, do you love me more than these?"

John 21:15

The Christ
My child, you're not yet strong and wise in your love.

The Disciple
In what way, my Lord?

The Christ
Because you fall away from My purposes with little opposition and too eagerly seek comfort apart from Me. One who has strong love for Me stands firm against temptation and refuses to be persuaded by the Enemy.

One who wisely loves doesn't focus on the gifts of the loved one, but on the loved one alone. The love and loved one is of far more value than any gift. If you truly love Me, you love Me above any gift I give you.

But all's not lost, even when you think of others and other things more than Me. My good and sweet love which you sometimes sense, comes from the grace and is foretaste of the heavenly country. But do not depend on these sensations, for they come and go. But it's a sign of your virtue and great merit to strive against evil thoughts and suggestions of the devil.

So don't let strange fantasies disturb you, even if you don't know from where they come. Bravely keep your purpose and intentions upon me. It's not an illusion when you are lifted up with heavenly thoughts and then suddenly brought down with earthly desires. These thoughts come involuntarily—not deliberately. So, as long as they displease you and you quickly put them out of your mind, you will do well and suffer no loss.

The Imitation of Christ, Book 3, Chapter 6

24

Overcoming Temptation

Thomas à Kempis

The temptations in your life are no different from what others experience. And God is faithful. He will not allow the temptation to be more than you can stand. When you are tempted, he will show you a way out so that you can endure.

First Corinthians 10:13

The Christ

Beware that your ancient Enemy strives to hinder your pursuit after good and to deter you from spiritual disciplines such as meditating on the good works of My saints, the serious remembrance of My death and resurrection, the forgiveness of your sins, the keeping of your heart and mind pure, and the desire to grow more like Me. The Enemy may work by suggesting evil thoughts and wearing you down with fatigue and fear, so he can keep you away from prayer and holy reading. Humble confession displeases the Enemy, and he wants to keep you from Holy Communion. Don't believe or pay attention to him when he tries to snare you with his lies.

Confront him when he suggests evil and unclean thoughts. Say to him, "Depart, unclean spirit. Cower in shame, you miserable one. You are horribly evil for bringing such things to my mind. Depart from me, detestable deceiver. You will have no part of me, but Jesus will be with me as a strong warrior, and you will be defeated. Stand down and be silent. Even though you plan more traps against me, I will not listen anymore. 'The LORD is my light and my salvation—so why should I be afraid? . . . Though a mighty army surrounds me, my heart will not be afraid' (Ps. 27:1, 3). The Lord is 'my rock and my redeemer' (19:14)."

Strive like a good soldier. And if sometimes you fail through weakness, summon up your strength more bravely than before. Trust in My more abundant grace, and avoid false confidence and pride. Because of pride, many are deceived and become blind. Let the ruin of the proud, who foolishly lift themselves up, be a continual warning and exhortation to be humble.

The Imitation of Christ, Book 3, Chapter 6

III

Obedience

And we can be sure that we know him if we obey his commandments. If someone claims, "I know God," but doesn't obey God's commandments, that person is a liar and is not living in the truth. But those who obey God's word truly show how completely they love him. That is how we know we are living in him. Those who say they live in God should live their lives as Jesus did.

First John 2:3–6

25. Loving Christ Demands Obeying Christ: *Catherine of Siena*
26. Obeying is the Key to the Kingdom: *Catherine of Siena*
27. Walking in the Light of Love: *Catherine of Siena*
28. Obeying with Humility: *Francis of Sales*
29. Loving Christ with Pure Motives: *Thomas à Kempis*
30. Working with Pure Motives: *Catherine of Siena*
31. Putting Christ's Teaching into Practice: *Thomas à Kempis*

25

Loving Christ Demands Obeying Christ

Catherine of Siena

"So why do you keep calling me 'Lord, Lord!' when you don't do what I say?"

Jesus, Luke 6:46

The Father

Your whole faith is founded upon obedience, for by it you prove your faithfulness to Me. As My Son taught, you must obey My commandments, the most important of which are to love Me above everything, and your neighbor as yourself.

These commandments are so inseparable, that you cannot observe or disobey one without observing or disobeying them all. Everyone who observes this principal commandment observes all the others. They are faithful to Me and their neighbor, for they love Me and My creations. For My sake, they endure every labor with humble patience—even if their neighbor isn't neighborly. This obedience is so excellent that you all derive grace from it, just as from disobedience you all derive death.

And so it is not enough to have My words; they must be put into practice. Obedience is the key that opens heaven. The Son placed this key in the hands of His apostles, who placed it in the hands of all who received Him through baptism. They promised to obey and renounce the world in all of its earthly splendor and delights. So, each person has in his hand the same key My Son had. The key with faith opens the gate of heaven. Yes, heaven has been opened by My Son, but each person must unlock it for themselves.

And so, take the key of obedience in your hand and walk by the commands of My Son. Do not love finite things, as do fools who follow the first man Adam. Don't follow his example of casting the key of obedience in the mud of impurity, breaking it with the hammer of pride, and corroding it with self-love. The key would have been entirely destroyed if My one and only Son, the Word, had not come. He took the key of obedience out of the mud with His hands, cleansed it with His blood, and purified it in the fire of divine love. He straightened it with justice and hammered your wickedness into shape on the anvil of His own body. He so perfectly repaired the key that no matter how much a man may have spoiled his key by his free will, he can repair it with grace using the same instruments that were used by My Word.

The Dialogue of Saint Catherine of Siena

26

Obeying is the Key to the Kingdom

Catherine of Siena

Since God chose you to be the holy people he loves, you must clothe yourselves with tenderhearted mercy, kindness, humility, gentleness, and patience. . . . Above all, clothe yourselves with love, which binds us all together in perfect harmony.

Colossians 3:12, 14

The Father

Oh, blinder than blind people who have damaged the key of obedience that opens the door of heaven! Do you think the disobedience that closed the door will open it? Or that the pride that caused you to fall can make you rise again? Do you think you will be admitted to the marriage feast in foul and filthy wedding apparel? Do you think that sitting down and binding yourself with the chain of deadly sin, you can walk? Or without a key that you can open the door? Do not imagine that you can, for it is a fantastic fallacy!

You must obey My Son's commandments. Leave behind sin by confession, sorrow of heart, and determination to live a holy life. Then you will throw off that hideous and defiled garment and be clothed in the shining wedding robe. Hurry with the key of obedience in your hand and open the door. But secure this key with the cord of humility as well as hatred of your past sins and contempt for the world. Fasten it with the love of pleasing Me, your Creator. Tie it around your waist so you need not fear losing it.

Be warned, My child, many take up this key of obedience. They have seen by the light of faith that in no other way can they escape eternal damnation. But they hold it in their hand without tying it around their waist with the cord of humility and hatred of their past sins and contempt for the world. And so, they are not perfectly clothed with My pleasure, but still seek to please themselves. They do not wear the cord of self-contempt, for they do not desire to be despised, but rather take delight in the praise of men.

And so, they are apt to lose their key. They will suffer a little extra fatigue, perhaps mental or physical trouble. As often happens, the hand of holy desire loosens its grasp and loses the key. They can indeed find it again—if they wish—while they live, but if they don't wish for it they will never find it.

Oh, how sweet and glorious is this virtue! O blessed obedience! You are conformed to My one and only Son, the Word. You are dwelling in the love of your neighbor, being anointed with true humility, which saves you from coveting his possessions which is contrary to My will. You walk upright, without bending, loving generously for your heart is sincere and not false. You are truly My children. Your kingdom is so great that no one can rule you, for you have come out of deadly slavery to your own sensuality, which destroyed your dignity. And having slain this enemy with hatred and dislike of your own pleasure, you have re-obtained your liberty.

The Dialogue of Saint Catherine of Siena

27

Walking in the Light of Love

Catherine of Siena

Those who obey God's commandments remain in fellowship with him, and he with them. And we know he lives in us because the Spirit he gave us lives in us.

First John 3:24

The Father

My dearest child, in My goodness and power I have repaired the key of obedience. But worldly people, lacking any good, do what's opposite to My virtue. Like unbridled horses without the bit of obedience, they go from bad to worse, from sin to sin, from misery to misery, from darkness to darkness, from death to death, until they finally reach the edge of the ditch of death. If they would listen to their gnawing conscience, they could obey My laws, but because of their long habit of sin, it is very hard for them to do so.

Therefore, let no one put off finding of the key of obedience to the moment of his death. Although, we have hope that they can repent and obey while they still have life, they should not delay repentance. What is the reason of all this, and of the blindness that prevents them recognizing this treasure of obedience?

To the contrary, My beloved children are obedient to My law and rejoice in My eternal vision with the pure and humble Lamb, the Maker of all things, and the Fulfiller and Giver of this law. By observing My law in this life, they taste peace without any disturbance. They are clothed in the most perfect peace, for they possess every good without any evil, safety without any fear, riches without any poverty, satisfaction without guilt, light without darkness, one supreme infinite good, shared by all those who taste it truly. What has placed them in so blessed a state? The blood of the Lamb, by whose goodness the key of obedience has lost its corrosion, so that, by the virtue of the blood, it has been able to unlock the door.

Take, then, the key of obedience with the light of faith. No longer walk in the cold and dark, but observe obedience in the fire of love, so that you may taste eternal life together with the other observers of the law.

The Dialogue of Saint Catherine of Siena

28

Obeying with Humility

Francis of Sales

Observe the requirements of the LORD your God, and follow all his ways. Keep the decrees, commands, regulations, and laws written in the Law of Moses so that you will be successful in all you do and wherever you go.

First Kings 2:3

Love alone leads to perfection, but the three main ways to acquire it are obedience, purity, and poverty. Obedience is a dedication of our hearts, purity of our bodies, and poverty of worldly goods to the love and service of God. These are the three members of the spiritual cross, and all three must be raised upon the fourth, which is humility.

Let us then strive to practice these three virtues in whatever situation we find ourselves. In this life, we may not attain the state of holy perfection, but we can practice them and become more perfect in our love for God and our neighbor.

Necessary Obedience

There are two kinds of obedience: one necessary, the other voluntary. The first includes a humble obedience to church leaders. We are also bound to government authorities—kings and magistrates—as well as domestic superiors such as fathers and mothers. Such obedience is necessary, because no one can free himself from the duty of obeying these superiors since God has appointed them to bear rule over us.

Therefore, obey their commands as far as love and wisdom will allow. Obey in things that are hard, disagreeable and inconvenient, for in doing so is found perfect obedience. And obey quietly, without objecting; promptly, without delay; cheerfully, without reluctance; and, above all, render a loving obedience for My Son's sake, who became obedient even to the death of the cross for your sake.

And while we are acquiring an eager obedience to superiors, we must yield and defer to our equals, giving way to their opinions where nothing wrong is involved, without arguing or being harsh. And fulfill the desires of those in positions below you as far as you reasonably can. Do not exercise stern authority over them, so long as they do well.

Voluntary Obedience

We undertake voluntary obedience when, by our own choice, we put ourselves under the authority of a member of the clergy, an accountability partner, or a counselor. This is not imposed by superiors. People do not choose their own king, bishop, or parents, but many people choose a spiritual guide. And whether a person takes a vow to obey the direction or simply agrees to consider the advice, all such obedience is voluntary, because it depends upon our own will.

Seek to be directed in your spiritual life by someone who is greatly respected, so that you will have double grace and virtue from their godly influence.

Blessed indeed are the obedient, for God will never permit them to go astray.

Introduction to the Devout Life, Part 3, Chapter 11

29

Loving Christ with Pure Motives

Thomas à Kempis

Loving God means keeping his commandments, and his commandments are not burdensome.

First John 5:3

Jesus has many lovers of His heavenly kingdom but few bearers of His cross. He has many seekers of comfort but few willing to face troubles and trial. He finds many companions at His table but few with Him in fasting. Many desire to rejoice with Him, but few are willing to undergo adversity for His sake. Many follow Jesus that they may eat of His bread, but few are willing to drink of the cup of His passion. Many are astonished at His miracles, but few follow after the shame of His cross.

Many love Jesus so long as no troubles happen to them. Many praise Him and bless Him, so long as they receive comforts from Him. But if Jesus hides Himself and seems to withdraw from them for even a little while, they immediately begin complaining or feel a great sense of dejection.

But those who love Jesus for Jesus' sake—and not for the comforts He gives to them—praise Him in all suffering and sorrow just as they do in the greatest blessings. And if He should never give them another blessing, they would nevertheless continue to always praise Him and give Him thanks.

Oh, how powerful is the pure love of Jesus—unmixed with any material benefits or love of self! Shouldn't all those constantly seeking His blessing be called mercenaries? Don't those who are always seeking their own gain and advantage show themselves to be lovers of themselves more than lovers of Christ? Who can be found who is willing to serve God altogether for no earthly benefit?

The Imitation of Christ, Book 2, Chapter 11

30

Working with Pure Motives

Catherine of Sienna

But the Holy Spirit produces this kind of fruit in our lives: love, joy, peace, patience, kindness, goodness, faithfulness, gentleness, and self-control. There is no law against these things!

Galatians 5:22–23

The Father

I have appointed you to labor in the vineyard of obedience in different ways. All My workers will receive a wage, not according to the work done or the length of time for which they served, but according to the measure of their love.

Many take their place of work in the vineyard as children. Some enter later in life, and others in old age. Sometimes these later laborers work with the fire of love, seeing the shortness of the time. They may surpass the work done by those who entered in childhood, who advanced slowly. By love of obedience, My workers receive their wages: having their hearts filled with the ocean of My eternal peace.

There are many whose obedience is so prompt, they obey before a command is given. They understand My intention before I say a word. They obey My intention rather than My words because they are one with Us. Therefore, the command comes, not from a word but from My character.

How are My children guided? By obedience, with the light of the most holy faith. By this light, they have slain and thrown aside their humbled self-will. By being obedient to Me and their spiritual leaders, they have navigated the tempestuous sea of this life with calm and serene mind as well as a tranquil heart. Obedience and faith have taken all darkness from them. They remain strong and firm, having lost all weakness and fear. They have overcome self-will, from which comes all weakness and fear.

Those who obey Me speak words of peace throughout all their life and at death receive eternal life. They receive eternal peace, tranquility, and rest. This goodness is impossible to comprehend. No one can value or understand it. It is infinitely good and cannot be understood by anything smaller than itself. A ship dipped into the sea, doesn't comprehend the whole ocean, but only what it can now see. The sea alone contains itself. Only I, the ocean of infinite peace, can truly comprehend and value it. And I rejoice in My own estimate and comprehension of My goodness. I don't leave you empty, but I share

Myself with you, filling you with perfect blessings. All My children comprehend and know My goodness in the measure in which it is given to them.

And so, My obedient children, the light of faith in the Truth burns in the furnace of My love. I have anointed you with humility and overpowered you with the sacrifice of Christ. Along with your patience and with self-sacrifice, strength, enduring perseverance, and all the other virtues, you receive your reward from Me, your Creator.

The Dialogue of Saint Catherine of Siena

31

Putting Christ's Teaching into Practice

Thomas à Kempis

But don't just listen to God's word. You must do what it says. Otherwise, you are only fooling yourselves. For if you listen to the word and don't obey, it is like glancing at your face in a mirror. You see yourself, walk away, and forget what you look like. But if you look carefully into the perfect law that sets you free, and if you do what it says and don't forget what you heard, then God will bless you for doing it.

James 1:22–25

The Lord promises, "the Kingdom of God is already among you" (Luke 17:21). If we turn our hearts to the Lord and forsake this miserable world, we will find rest for our souls. We must learn to despise outward things and give ourselves to inward things. Then we will see the kingdom of God come within us. For the kingdom of God is peace and joy in the Holy Spirit, but it's not given to the unrighteous.

Christ will come to us and comfort us, if we prepare a worthy home for Him within us. All His glory and beauty are from within, and that's where He is pleased to dwell. He often visits inward people and makes His sweet presence known with spiritual words, comfort, much peace, and exceedingly wonderful friendship.

Faithful souls, we must prepare our hearts for Jesus, our bridegroom, that He may graciously come to us and dwell within us. He says, "All who love me will do what I say. My Father will love them, and we will come and make our home with each of them" (John 14:23). Therefore, let's open our hearts to Him and refuse entrance to all others. When we have Christ, we are rich and have no needs. He will be our provider and faithful protector in all things, so that we have no need to trust in humans, for they soon change and swiftly pass away. But Christ remains with us forever and firmly stands beside us even to the end.

We can't put our trust in frail, mortal people, even though they may be helpful and dear to us. Neither should we get too upset if sometimes they oppose and contradict us. Those who are on our side today, may be against us tomorrow. They can turn like the wind. So, we must put our whole trust in God, and let Him have our respect and love. He Himself will answer for us and will do for us what is best. "For this world is not our permanent home; we are looking forward to a home yet to come" (Heb. 13:14). We will never have rest unless we are closely united to Christ within us.

Why do we look here and there for satisfaction, since this is not our place of rest? Our home is in heaven, and we should look at all earthly things as if they were only passing by. All things pass away and we also with them. Don't cling to earthly things for they—and we—may be taken away and perish. Let our thoughts be on the Most High and desires continually focused on Christ. We can't behold high and heavenly things, but we can rest in the thought of His death and resurrection. We can meditate on His wounds inflicted for our eternal life in heaven. In the precious marks of the nails and the spear, we will find great comfort in our troubles. As we look upon the sights of this wicked world, we will have His peace and will easily bear the world's unkind words.

If it is well with us and we have been purified from evil, all things work together for our good and profit. However, if many things displease and often trouble us, then we are not perfectly dead to our selfish desires and impure love for created things. If we will reject outward comfort, we will be able to contemplate heavenly things and enjoy inward joy.

The Imitation of Christ, Book 2, Chapter 1

IV

Solitude

Jesus often withdrew to the wilderness for prayer.

Luke 5:16

32

Being Held in Love's Embrace

John of the Cross

Be still, and know that I am God!

Psalm 46:10

In deepest solitude
I found the narrow way:
a secret giving such release
that I was stunned and stammering
rising above all earthly knowledge.
You looked with love upon me
And deep within Your eyes imprinted grace.
This mercy set me free,
Held in Your love's embrace,
To lift my eyes adoring
to Your grace.

From *I Came into the Unknowing*

How gently and lovingly
You wake in my heart,
where in secret You dwell alone;
and in Your sweet breathing,
filled with good and glory
how tenderly You dwell in my heart
with love.

From *The Spiritual Canticle*

Let us rejoice, Beloved,
Let us go forth
To behold ourselves
In Your Beauty.

From *The Living Flame of Love*

33

Finding Our Place of Solitude

Francis of Sales

Then Jesus said, "Let's go off by ourselves to a quiet place and rest awhile." He said this because there were so many people coming and going that Jesus and his apostles didn't even have time to eat.

Mark 6:31

If you wish to live a godly life, don't seek or ignore society. To seek simply being out and about is as bad as indifference or contempt for our neighbors. We are told to love our neighbors as ourselves, so to love them, we can't avoid being with them. But, the test of loving one's self is to be happy when alone.

Social interactions can benefit or harm our spiritual lives. We must avoid groups bent on evil or engaging in actions that are mean-spirited, sensual, materialistic, or wasteful. Turn away from these groups and people like a bee from a manure pile. Above all, avoid close relationships with those whose devotion to God is weak or unstable.

Finally, there is a profitable society. It will always be very good when we meet with good, devout people. Vines grown amid olive trees will bear richer grapes, and when we fellowship with godly people, we drink in some of their goodness. The bumblebee can't make honey alone, but works together with other bees. Our own spiritual life will be enriched by close relationships with other devout souls.

But there are times we must regularly shun society for our spiritual well-being. I'm not speaking of that mental solitude in which we can escape in our spirit even while in a large crowd. No, it is important to have regular time of physically escaping from society into solitude. I'm not suggesting we escape to the desert like the apostle Paul or the other hermits and desert disciples. It is well to escape to our own room, a garden, or closet where we can best collect our thoughts and refresh our souls with good and holy thoughts from Scripture and other spiritual readings.

Solitude is so very important, my children, for it is one of the surest means of spiritual progress. Throughout the day, we can place ourselves in God's presence by recalling Scripture or other readings. Consider what God does and what you are doing. Imagine His eyes always focusing on you with incomparable love. "O my God," you will cry out. "Why can't I always be looking toward you even as you are looking upon me? Why do I think so little about you? O my soul, my only resting place is God, and yet how often do I wander off?"

The birds have nests in lofty trees, and the deer has his refuge in the thick woods where he can find shelter from the sun's burning heat. In the same way, my children, our hearts ought to have a daily resting place where we can escape to seek a break and refreshment in our busy schedules. It will be a fortress, protected from temptation. Blessed indeed is the soul who can truly say, "You, Lord, are my refuge, my castle, my solid rock, my shelter from the storm, and heat of the day."

Be sure then, my children, that while we're externally occupied with family, business, and social duties, we frequently and regularly escape to the solitude within our heart.

Introduction to the Devout Life, Part 3, Chapter 12

34

Finding Solitude in Our Crowded Lives

Francis of Sales

Let all that I am wait quietly before God,
for my hope is in him.

Psalm 62:5

As I previously wrote, remember the supreme importance of solitude with our Lord and Savior.

Solitude doesn't need to be hindered in any way by the crowds that surround us—they surround our bodies but not our souls. Our hearts remain alone in the sole presence of God. This is what David sought in the midst of his many responsibilities as king of Israel. The Psalms are full of expressions such as, "Yet I still belong to you; you hold my right hand" (Ps. 73:23). "I lift my eyes to you, O God, enthroned in heaven. We keep looking to the LORD our God for his mercy" (123:1–2).

There are few social duties so important as to prevent a regular retreat of the heart into this sacred solitude. When Catherine of Sienna's parents deprived her of any place or time for prayer and meditation, our Lord inspired her with the thought of making an interior chapel in her mind. There she could enjoy holy solitude in the midst of her outward duties. So, when the world assaulted her, she could remain unaffected because she could retire within her secret retreat and find comfort with her heavenly Bridegroom.

So, she counseled her spiritual daughters to make a refuge within their hearts in which to dwell. In this way, we can withdraw into our inward retreat where we lay our soul bare, face to face with God. David writes about this: "I am like an owl in the desert, / like a little owl in a far-off wilderness. / I lie awake, / lonely as a solitary bird on the roof" (Ps. 102:6–7). David made a habit of retreating like a bird for solitude and contemplation.

Elzear was a godly lay member of the Franciscan Order as well as a civic leader, diplomat, and military leader. When he had been long separated from his righteous and beloved wife Delphine, she sent a messenger to inquire about him and his welfare. Elzear wrote in reply: "I am well, dear wife, and if you would see me, seek me at the wounded side of our dear Lord Jesus; that is my sure dwelling place, and elsewhere you will seek me in vain." Surely, he was a true Christian soldier who spoke in this manner.

Introduction to the Devout Life, Part 2, Chapter 12

35

Praying by Listening

Francis of Sales

"But when you pray, go away by yourself, shut the door behind you, and pray to your Father in private. Then your Father, who sees everything, will reward you."

Jesus, Matthew 6:6

Prayer opens our minds to the brightness of divine light and our wills to the warmth of heavenly love. Nothing is more effective in purifying our minds from ignorance or our wills from unrighteous desires. It is healing water which causes the roots of our good desires to send forth fresh shoots, which wash away our souls' imperfections and dispels the thirst of human desires.

I especially recommend sincere silent prayer to you, especially prayer that focuses on the life, death, and resurrection of our Lord. If we frequently contemplate Him in meditation, our whole soul will be filled with Him. We will grow in His likeness, and our actions will reflect His. He is the Light of the World, so in Him, by Him, and for Him we will be enlightened and illuminated. He is the Tree of Life, beneath the shadow where we must find rest. He is the living Fountain of Jacob's well, from which we may wash away every stain.

Children learn to talk by hearing their mother speak and trying to imitate her with stammering childish sounds. We must cling to the Savior in meditation: Listening to His Word and watching His actions and intentions in the Gospels. We will learn in time, through His grace, to speak, act, and think like Christ Himself.

Believe me, my children, there is no way to God except through this door. Just as the glass of a mirror would give no reflection except for the metal behind it, so neither can we here below contemplate the Godhead, without being united to the holy humanity of our Savior. His life and death are the best, sweetest, and most profitable subjects that we can possibly select for meditation. It is so meaningful that the Savior calls Himself the Bread of Life which has come down from heaven. Just as we eat bread with all kinds of other food, so we need to meditate and feed upon our dear Lord in every prayer and action.

Devote a regular time each day, preferably early in the morning, when your mind will be fresh and less cluttered after the night's rest. Begin all prayer, whether silently or out loud, by focusing on the presence of God. If you observe this discipline strictly, you will soon see how useful it is.

It may help to read the Apostles' Creed or the Lord's Prayer. Study them diligently, and thoroughly examine the meaning of these holy words. We must steadily fix our thoughts on the purpose of the words. Don't attempt to say many words, but seek to say a few with your whole heart. One "Our Father" uttered devoutly is worth more than many prayers hurried over.

Introduction to the Devout Life, Part 2, Chapter 1

36

Praying Short Prayers

Author of The Cloud of Unknowing

"When you pray, don't babble on and on as the Gentiles do. They think their prayers are answered merely by repeating their words again and again. Don't be like them, for your Father knows exactly what you need even before you ask him!"

Jesus, Matthew 6:7–8

Just as God, by His grace, brings thoughts into our minds suddenly, without any preparation, so our prayers come in the same way. The prayers of the church, written and ordained by our holy fathers, are well and good, but special prayers always rise spontaneously.

This occurs very naturally. For example, when we are overcome by fear in the presence of a sudden emergency such as fire, a person dying, or any other trauma, we naturally cry out from our intensity of feelings for help to come at once. And how do we do this? Certainly, not in many words with many syllables. The reason is simple. It would take us too long if we tried to explain the nature of the need.

So we cry out suddenly with great urgency a little one-syllable word, such as "fire" or "help."

This little word immediately pierces the ears of the hearers and motivates action. In the same way, a little word of one syllable—whether spoken or thought—reaches the depth of the spirit. This depth is height, for spiritually all is one, height and depth, length and breadth. It pierces the ears of the almighty God more than does any of the Psalms or written prayers thoughtlessly mumbled through one's lips. This is the reason it is written that a short prayer pierces heaven.

The Cloud of Unknowing, Chapter 37

Prayer, properly understood, is simply a devout desire directed toward God to accept what is good and remove what is evil. Since all evil is considered either sin by its action or character, we can fervently pray to remove evil by simply using only this little word—"sin." And if we wish to fervently pray to receive good, let us cry out in word or thought only this little word—"God." We do this because all good is in God by action or His character.

But don't study mere words, because you will never achieve your purpose in prayer that way. It is never achieved by study, but only by grace. And even though I've suggested these two words—sin and God—you must never pray with any words at all unless they are inspired by God.

Even though brevity of prayer is greatly recommended here, we do not place any limit on the frequency of prayer. We must pray prayers in the Spirit's timing. This means that it should never cease until it receives all that it is seeking.

The Cloud of Unknowing, Chapter 39

37

Praying Scripture

Ignatius of Loyola

I pray that from his glorious, unlimited resources he will empower you with inner strength through his Spirit. Then Christ will make his home in your hearts as you trust in him.

Ephesians 3:16–17

We may pray kneeling or seated, whichever most conducive to a spiritual and devout attitude. We may keep our eyes closed or fixed on a meaningful object or place. To prevent our minds from wandering, consider these outlines for prayer:

Praying the Ten Commandments

For the first method of prayer, it is well to meditate on the Ten Commandments. Begin with the first, asking, "How have I kept it and in what way I have failed?" Spend adequate time. If during this time, we find faults, then ask pardon and forgiveness for them. Let this same method be followed on each one of the Ten Commandments.

If we consider a commandment and find no habit of sinning, we don't need to delay. But if we find one on which we more or less stumble, continue praying about it. We should carefully consider and examine ourselves, and confess any sins found. Then ask for grace and God's help to make any changes.

We can observe the same manner of prayer regarding the seven deadly sins: pride, greed, anger, envy, lust, over-eating, and laziness.

The Spiritual Exercises of St. Ignatius of Loyola,
Three Methods of Prayer: Method One

Praying the Lord's Prayer

The second method of prayer involves reciting the Lord's Prayer, word by word, concentrating on each individual word. Look for meanings and comparisons. Find comfort and conviction inspired by each word. We can do the same for other prayers and Scripture passages, turning them into our personal prayers.

The Spiritual Exercises of St. Ignatius of Loyola,
Three Methods of Prayer: Method Two

V

Meditation

Oh, the joys of those who do not
follow the advice of the wicked,
or stand around with sinners,
or join in with mockers.
But they delight in the law of the Lord*,*
meditating on it day and night.

Psalm 1:1–2

38. Placing Ourselves in the Presence of God: *Francis of Sales*
39. Reflecting on What We Owe Christ: *Teresa of Avila*
40. Filling Our Soul with Living Water: *Teresa of Avila*
41. Focusing on One Thing: *Author of* The Cloud of Unknowing
42. Meditating on Our Purpose and God's Plan: *Francis of Sales*
43. Putting into Practice What We Learn: *Francis of Sales*
44. Raising Our Thoughts to God and Heavenly Things: *Francis of Sales*
45. Maintaining Devotions When We Have No Desire: *Francis of Sales*
46. Coming Down from the Mountaintop: *Francis of Sales*

Note: Biblical meditation is the very opposite of Eastern meditation. The Psalms call for filling our minds with thoughts of God and His glory; Eastern meditation concentrates on emptying one's mind to attain nothingness.

38

Placing Ourselves in the Presence of God

Francis of Sales

I will meditate on your majestic, glorious splendor and your wonderful miracles.

Psalm 145:5

Meditation is very neglected today. The practice of mental prayer—as opposed to vocal prayer—is very close to meditation in that both draw our minds and spirits into the presence of God. So, I will give you a short and easy method for using it.

First of all, the preparation for meditating on God consists of two points: first, placing ourselves in the presence of God, and second, asking for His aid. To place ourselves in His presence, I will suggest four chief considerations which you can use at first.

First, a sincere awareness that His presence is universal. He is everywhere and in all, and there is no place, nowhere in the world, devoid of His most holy presence. So, even as birds on the wing meet the air continually, let us go where we will and meet with that Presence that is always everywhere.

We can believe this, but we don't always comprehend its importance. A blind man, when in the presence of his king, will display a reverential demeanor if told that the king is there, although he's unable to see him. But practically, what we do not see we easily forget, and so we readily lapse into carelessness and irreverence.

In the same way, we do not see our God. Although faith promises us that He is present, we are unable to see Him with our earthly eyes. We are too apt to forget Him or act as if He were far away. So, even though we perfectly know that He is everywhere, we don't keep it in mind nor act as if He is indeed everywhere.

And so, before we begin to pray, we need to always remind ourselves of His faithful presence. This is what David meant when he exclaimed, "I can never escape from your Spirit! / I can never get away from your presence! / If I go up to heaven, you are there; / if I go down to the grave, you are there" (Ps. 139:7–8).

In the same way, Jacob, beholding the ladder which went up to heaven, cried out, "Surely the Lord is in this place, and I wasn't even aware of it!" (Gen. 28:16). Surely, Jacob could not have failed to know that God was everywhere and in all things, but he had not fully comprehended this truth. So, when we are preparing to pray, we must meditate with our whole hearts, "God is indeed here."

The second way of placing ourselves in the Lord's sacred presence is to meditate on the profound truth that He is not only present in the place where we are, but that He is present in our very hearts and minds! He ignites and inspires us with His holy presence, abiding there as Heart of our hearts, Spirit of our spirits. Our soul animates our whole body and therefore every member of it, but it dwells especially in our hearts. So, while God is present everywhere, yet He makes His intimate dwelling within our spirit. Therefore, Asaph, David's minister of music, proclaims, "God remains the strength of my heart" (Ps. 73:26), and Paul writes, "For in him we live and move and exist" (Acts 17:28). Dwell upon this thought until you have kindled a great reverence within your heart for God who is so closely present to you.

The third way is to think upon how our Lord thinks of us. In His ascended humanity, He looks down upon all people, but most particularly on all Christians, because they are above all His children. He keeps watch over all who pray. This is not mere imagination, but the very real truth.

The fourth way is simply to exercise our ordinary imagination, picturing our Savior in His sacred humanity as if He were beside you, just as we may think of our friends and imagine that we see and hear them at our side.

Make use of one or another of these methods for comprehending yourself in the presence of God before you begin to pray.

Introduction to the Devout Life, Part 2, Chapter 2

39

Reflecting on What We Owe Christ

Teresa of Avila

But then I recall all you have done, O Lord;
I remember your wonderful deeds of long ago.
They are constantly in my thoughts.
I cannot stop thinking about your mighty works.

Psalm 77:11–12

If we don't comprehend to whom we are speaking, although we may be saying many words, I don't consider it prayer. Sometimes, indeed, we do pray devoutly without acknowledging to whom we are addressing. The custom of speaking to God Almighty as freely as with a servant—not caring at all whether the words are suitable or not, but simply saying the first thing that comes to mind, or quoting from prayers we learned by rote—cannot be called prayer.

God grant that no Christian may address Him in this manner. I trust His majesty will prevent any of us from praying this way!

The Interior Castle, The First Mansions, Chapter 1

If we never look up at Christ and reflect on what we owe Him for having died for us, I don't understand how we can know Him or perform good deeds in His service. What value is there in faith without works? And what are they worth if they are not united to the merits of Jesus Christ, our only good? What would motivate us to love our Lord unless we thought of Him? May He give us grace to understand how much we cost Him. "The servant is not above his lord"; so we must serve Him if we want to enjoy His glory. And prayer is what is necessary to prevent us from constantly falling into temptation.

The Interior Castle, The Second Mansions, Chapter 1

40

Filling Our Soul with Living Water

Teresa of Avila

"Anyone who is thirsty may come to me! Anyone who believes in me may come and drink! For the Scriptures declare, 'Rivers of living water will flow from his heart.'"

Jesus, John 7:37–38

Let us imagine we see two fountains with basins which fill with water.

These two basins are filled in different ways: the one with water from a distant spring flowing into it through many pipes and waterworks, while the other basin is built near the source of the spring itself and fills quite noiselessly.

If the fountain is plentiful, like the one we speak of, after the basin is full the water overflows in a great stream which flows continually. No machinery is needed here, nor does the water run through aqueducts. Such is the difference between the two kinds of prayer.

The water running through the pipes resembles sensible devotion, which is obtained by meditation. We gain it by our thoughts, by meditating on created things, and by the labor of our minds; in short, it is the result of our endeavors, while profiting the soul.

The other fountain, like divine comforts, receives the water from the source itself, which signifies God. As usual, when He in His majesty desires to bless us with supernatural favors, we experience the greatest peace, calm, and sweetness in the inmost depths of our being. We don't know where or how this happens.

This joy is not like earthly happiness. It is at once felt by the heart after gradually filling it to the brim. This delight overflows throughout all our spirit, until at last it reaches the body. Therefore, I say it arises from God and ends in ourselves, for whoever experiences it will find that the whole physical part of our nature shares in this delight and sweetness.

This is not a thing we can imagine or gain by anything we can do. Clearly, it doesn't arise from the base metal of human nature, but from the most pure gold of divine wisdom. I believe that in this case, the powers of the soul are not merely united to God, but are absorbed and astounded at the marvel before them. I believe that in this case the will must in some way be united with that of God. The after effects on the soul, and the subsequent behavior of the person, show whether this prayer was genuine or not. Living out our experiences is the best crucible by which to test it.

Though we may meditate and try our hardest, and though we shed tears to gain it, we can't make this water flow. God alone gives it to whom He chooses, and often when the soul is least thinking of it. We are His, brothers and sisters, so let Him do what He will with us, and lead us where He will. We must sincerely humble and sacrifice ourselves to His will, not only in our imagination—which often deceives us—but in rejecting all selfish things. Then, our Lord will not only grant us these favors but many others that we do not know even how to desire. May He be forever praised and blessed! Amen.

The Interior Castle, The Fourth Mansions, Chapter 2

41

Focusing on One Thing

Author of The Cloud of Unknowing

As Jesus and the disciples continued on their way to Jerusalem, they came to a certain village where a woman named Martha welcomed him into her home. Her sister, Mary, sat at the Lord's feet, listening to what he taught. But Martha was distracted by the big dinner she was preparing.

Luke 10:38–40

It seems to me that those who choose to sit at the feet of Jesus, like Mary, should not only forgive those like Martha but all those who are constantly busy for Jesus and complaining about those who seem to be lost in contemplation. We should be so occupied with spiritual things that we pay little attention to what others say or do. That was what Mary, who is the example for all of us, did when her sister Martha complained to our Lord. And if we will truly do the same, our Lord will do the same for us now as He did for Mary then.

And what was that? Our beloved Lord Jesus Christ, from whom no secret thing is hidden, was asked by Martha to act as judge and to order Mary to stand up and help her serve Him. He perceived, however, that Mary was fervently occupied in spirit with her love for Him and His divinity. So He kindly replied, as was His character, that Mary didn't need to leave her position of listening to and loving Him.

And how did Jesus answer? Certainly not as a judge, as Martha asked Him to do, but as an advocate defending Mary's act of love. "Martha, Martha!" He said twice for emphasis. He spoke her name, as He wanted her to hear Him and obey His words. "You are very busy," He said, "and are troubled about many things." There are active people who need to be busy constantly and be doing many different things, first for their own use, and then in deeds of mercy for their fellow Christians as charity requires. But Jesus wanted Martha to know that serving Him was good and beneficial for the health of her soul. But He also told her that she was not engaged in the best work. "Only one thing is necessary."

And what is that one thing? That God should be loved and praised above all other things physical or spiritual that a person may do. Jesus warned Martha that she should not think that she could both love God and praise Him above all other things physical or spiritual, *and* be busy at the same time with the necessities of this life. He wanted to free her from the guilt of not being able to serve God perfectly in both physical and spiritual affairs. She could schedule time for both! He added that Mary had chosen the best part, and that this would never be taken away from her. The reason is that this perfect stirring of love that begins here in this life is equal with that which shall last eternally in the bliss of heaven, for they both are one.

The Cloud of Unknowing, Chapter 20

42

Meditating on Our Purpose and God's Plan

Francis of Sales

You go before me and follow me.
You place your hand of blessing on my head.
Such knowledge is too wonderful for me,
too great for me to understand!

Psalm 139:5–6

God did not bring us into the world because He had any need of us—useless as we are—but solely that He might demonstrate His goodness in us, giving us His glory and grace. And to this end, He gave us understanding that we might know Him; memory that we might think of Him; a will that we might love Him; imagination that we might appreciate His mercies; sight that we might behold the marvels of His works; speech that we might praise Him, and so on with all our other faculties.

Since we were created and placed in the world to demonstrate His goodness, all contrary actions should be shunned and rejected, as also we should avoid as idle and useless anything that doesn't promote God's glory.

Consider how unhappy are those who don't meditate on the things of God. They live as though they were created only to build and plant, to increase in riches, and to amuse themselves with worthless things.

With this in mind, we should humble ourselves if we have meditated so little on all of this. "My God, of what was I thinking when I did not think of You? What did I remember when I forgot You? What did I love when I failed to love You? I regret that when I should have been feeding on the truth, I was only filling myself with vanity and serving the world, which was made to serve me."

Let us detest our past life. May we renounce vain and useless thoughts, frivolous and hateful memories. May we renounce all unhealthy friendships, all unprofitable efforts, and miserably ungrateful self-indulgence, all pitiful compromises.

May we turn to God and pray:

> *You, my God and Savior, from now on You will be sole object of my thoughts; no more will I give my mind to ideas which are displeasing to You. All the days of my life I will meditate on the greatness of Your goodness, so lovingly poured out upon me. Forever more, You will be the delight of my heart, the resting place for all my love. From now on, I will hate and reject the vain pleasures and amusements, the empty pursuits which have absorbed my time— the unprofitable ties which have bound my heart.*

In summary:

1. Thank God, who has made you for so gracious a future. *"You have made us, O Lord for Yourself that we may enjoy eternally the immensity of Your glory. We will never be worthy of it or praise You as we should."*

2. Offer to our dearest Lord, all our loves and dreams with our whole heart and soul.

3. Pray. *"I beg You, O God, that You would accept my desires and longings, and give Your blessing to my soul. Enable me to fulfill them, through the merits of Your dear Son's precious blood shed upon the cross for me."*

Introduction to the Devout Life, Part 1, Chapter 10

43

Putting into Practice What We Learn

Francis of Sales

Study this Book of Instruction continually. Meditate on it day and night so you will be sure to obey everything written in it. Only then will you prosper and succeed in all you do.

Joshua 1:8

Above all things, when your time of meditation is ended strive to retain the thoughts and resolutions you have made. Earnestly practice them throughout the day. This is the real fruit of meditation. Without putting our meditation into practice, it will not only be unprofitable, but actually harmful. Meditating on virtues without practicing them puffs us up with unrealities, until we begin to believe that we are what we meditated upon and resolved to be. But on the contrary, our actions and attitudes will be hollow and dangerous rather than sincere and substantial. We must work diligently to carry out our resolutions and seek for all opportunities—great and small—to put them into practice. For instance, if our resolution was to win over those who oppose us by gentleness, seek throughout the day opportunities for treating such people kindly, and if they don't arise, strive to speak well of them and pray for them.

When we leave our place of meditation and prayer, we should retain our focus so the help received won't be scattered. We should try to maintain silence for a brief time and let our thoughts gradually shift from devotion to business, keeping alive as long as possible the insights and intentions inspired in our meditation.

Suppose we received a precious porcelain bottle filled with expensive perfume which we needed to carry home. We would walk very cautiously, not looking around, but watching carefully so as not to trip or stumble and spill any of the valuable fragrance.

Likewise, after meditation, we must not allow ourselves to be distracted, but look straight before us. Of course, as we go back to our family, job, school, or other responsibilities, we should treat those we meet with the love and compassion of God which we have just experienced. But try to carry as much of the precious perfume of your meditation into your daily life.

We should strive to make this transition from time alone with our Lord to our earthly labors easily and smoothly. Even if what we will be facing seems completely contrary to the loving thoughts just experienced, enter into the fray with prayer and the knowledge that the same Lord you met in meditation is with you this moment.

And so, the lawyer should be able to go from meditating on Christ to mediating a case, the tradesman to the shop, the parent to the cares of children, so calmly and gently as not to be in any way disturbed by doing so. In both meditation and the mundane, we are fulfilling God's will as we turn from one to the other in a devout and humble spirit.

Introduction to the Devout Life, Part 2, Chapter 8

44

Raising Our Thoughts to God and Heavenly Things

Francis of Sales

Help me understand the meaning of your commandments, and I will meditate on your wonderful deeds.

Psalm 119:27

Meditation is designed to raise our thoughts to God and heavenly things. Meditation differs from study and ordinary methods of thought which don't have as their goal the love of God or growth of holiness. So, meditation limits the efforts of our mind within the bounds of spiritual matters, such as Christ's character, teachings, or death and resurrection. Our mind dwells upon spiritual matters and finds sufficient insights, light, and fruit on which to rest and meditate, even as the bee hovers over one flower as long as it offers nectar. But if we do not find nectar to feed our mind after a reasonable effort, then we go on to another consideration. The key is to be quiet and listening, and not to be eager or hurried.

Introduction to the Devout Life, Part 2, Chapter 8

One part of meditation, but not necessary for all meditation, is called by some "local representation" or "an interior picture." It is simply imagining in vivid detail an event in the life of Christ as though we are eyewitnesses in the first century. For instance, if we wish to meditate upon our Lord on His cross, we would use our imagination to place ourselves on Mount Calvary, seeing and hearing all that occurred there during His passion. Or we might imagine ourselves as the disciples listening to the words of Christ. In the same way, you may imagine any subjects which involve visible, tangible circumstances. When it is a question of such abstract mysteries as God's greatness, His characteristics, the end of our creation, or other invisible things, you cannot practice this use of your imagination.

Introduction to the Devout Life, Part 2, Chapter 8

I would have us follow a very simple method, and not weary our minds with striving after elaborate, new imaginations. Still, often this use of the imagination tends to focus our minds on the mystery we wish to meditate. It prevents our thoughts from wandering here and there, just as we might shut a bird within a cage or fasten a hawk by its leg. Some people will tell you that it is better to confine yourself to mere abstract thoughts and a simple mental and spiritual consideration of these mysteries. This may, however, be too difficult for beginners, and until God calls you up higher, I would advise you contentedly dwell on the actions and teaching of Christ as I have pointed out.

Introduction to the Devout Life, Part 2, Chapter 4

45

Maintaining Devotions When We Have No Desire

Francis of Sales

I will study your commandments
and reflect on your ways.

Psalm 119:15

Sometimes it will happen that we have no desire for Christ, or gain any benefit from meditating on Him. Please don't be troubled, but instead simply seek relief in prayer. We should share our frustrations, confess our unworthiness before our Lord, plead for His aid, and say, like Jacob proclaimed to the heavenly being he was wrestling, "I will not let you go unless you bless me" (Gen. 32:26); or as the Gentile woman who begged the Jewish Jesus to heal her daughter, "Even dogs are allowed to eat the scraps that fall beneath their masters' table" (Matt. 15:27).

Or we can read from Scripture or a godly book until such time as our minds are calmed and enlivened. But if, after all this, we are still unrelieved of our spiritual dryness—however great it may be—we must continue striving to have a holy attitude in God's sight.

Many guests appear before a king without any word. They come and bow before the king to merely pay homage and to be in his presence. Likewise, we should appear before our King of Kings to worship Him and testify our loyalty. If it pleases God's divine majesty to speak to our hearts through the Holy Spirit, it is indeed a great honor and sweet to our soul. But if He does not grant us such a favor—and we have not felt His recognition of our presence before Him—nevertheless, we must not neglect our daily audience before Him. On the contrary, we must remain calmly and devoutly before Him. He is certain to recognize our patient waiting and notice our faithfulness and perseverance. Then, at another time, He will make His presence known and let us taste all the sweetness of holy meditation. But even if it is not so, let us be satisfied with the privilege of being in His presence and being seen by our great Lord and Savior.

Introduction to the Devout Life, Part 2, Chapter 9

46

Coming Down from the Mountaintop

Francis of Sales

. . . I will meditate continually on your decrees.

Psalm 119:117

We should conclude our meditation with three acts offered with the utmost humility.

First, an act of *thanksgiving*—thanking God for His love and any insights or inspirations that He has brought to our hearts and for His mercy and goodness in making His will known to us.

Second, an act of *sacrifice*—we offer back to God all the love and inspiration He has given us. For it is by His goodness and mercy, by the death and merits of His dear Son, that He has given us understanding.

The third act is one of *petition*—we ask God to give us a share in the righteousness of His dear Son, and His blessing and assistance that we may be able to put our insights and inspiration into practice. And pray for the church and all her ministers, your family and friends, and all others, using the Lord's Prayer as the most comprehensive and needful of prayers.

In addition to all this, I urge you gather a little bouquet of devotion. What I mean is this: When walking in a beautiful garden, most people want to gather a few flowers as they go, which they keep, and enjoy for their scent during the day. So, when our minds explore some mystery in meditation, it is well to pick out one or more points that have especially captured attention and are most likely to be helpful to us throughout the day. This should be written down at once before ending our time of meditation.

Introduction to the Devout Life, Part 2, Chapter 7

VI

Servanthood

"Anyone who wants to serve me must follow me, because my servants must be where I am. And the Father will honor anyone who serves me."

Jesus, John 12:26

47

Serving Selflessly

Julian of Norwich

Jesus replied, "The Scriptures say,
'You must worship the LORD your God
and serve only him.'"

Luke 4:8

While I was meditating, God showed me a picture and gave me understanding. I saw two people: our Lord and a servant. The Lord sat stately at rest and in peace. The servant reverently stood before his Lord, ready to do his Lord's will. The Lord lovingly and sweetly looked upon His servant and gently sent him on his way to do the Master's will. The servant obeyed quickly and ran in great haste, because he loved to do his Lord's will. But suddenly, the servant fell into a ravine and seriously injured himself. He wailed, moaning and groaning, and though he struggled, he was not able to stand up or move in any way.

And I understood that this injury symbolized the hurt of not being able to turn his head to his loving Lord for comfort. At the time, he was weak and unwise spiritually. He obsessed about his problems. However, he was filled with only goodwill and his desire to serve. He wasn't lazy but eager to stand before his Lord and do His will. So, in His love and righteousness, the Lord tenderly looked upon him.

And I saw the dual manner in which the Lord regarded His servant. One, outward, full of meek and mild empathy as well as grief for the servant's injury. And inwardly, spiritually, anticipating with joy and compassion in the restoration He will bring His servant by His generous grace.

And I saw in the servant, an inward knowledge that he should look up and worship his Lord, for this is the primary work of a servant. And the servant—having no regard for himself or his injury—stood up and continued on his way, worshipping his Lord as he accomplished his mission.

Revelation of Divine Love, Chapter 51

48

Serving with Humility

Francis of Assisi

Therefore, whenever we have the opportunity, we should do good to everyone—especially to those in the family of faith.

Galatians 6:10

That no one should take a position of superiority upon himself

"For even the Son of Man came not to be served but to serve others," says the Lord (Mark 10:45). Let those who are appointed over others glory in this superiority only as much as if they had been delegated to wash the feet of their brothers and sisters. And if they would be more upset by the loss of their superior position than they would be by losing the office of washing feet, then their good works and their own soul are in great danger.

That no one should glory except in the cross of the Lord

Consider how great a status of excellence the Lord has placed upon us, because He has created and formed us in the image of His beloved Son according to the body, and to His own likeness according to the Spirit. Yet all the creatures under heaven know, obey, and serve their Creator in their own way much better than we humans! Even the demons didn't crucify Him, but we together with them crucified Him and still crucify Him by taking delight in bad habits and sins. So, how can we glory in ourselves?

If we were so clever and wise that we possessed all scientific knowledge, and if we knew how to interpret every form of language, and could investigate heavenly things in every detail, we couldn't glory in that. There may be someone who has received from the Lord a special knowledge of sovereign wisdom, but one demon knows more of heavenly and earthly things than all men and women put together.

In the same way, if we were more handsome and beautiful, as well as richer than all others, and even if we could work wonders and put demons to flight, all these things would be hurtful to us. Nothing really belongs to us, and in nothing can we glory. The only things we may glory in are our weaknesses and the holy cross of our Lord Jesus Christ, which we daily bear.

Admonitions, Rules, Etc., Part 1

49

Serving Secretly

Francis of Assasi

"Whoever wants to be first among you must be the slave of everyone else. For even the Son of Man came not to be served but to serve others and to give his life as a ransom for many."

Jesus, Mark 10:44–45

Of the Humble Servant of God

Blessed is the servant who is no more puffed up because of what the good the Lord says and works through him any more than what God says and works through others. A man sins who wishes to receive more from his neighbor than he is himself is willing to give to the Lord God.

Of the Happy and Unhappy Servant

Blessed are the servants who give up all their goods to the Lord God, for those who retain anything for themselves hide "the master's money" (Matt. 25:18) and so "even what they think they understand will be taken away from them" (Luke 8:18).

Of the Good and Humble Servant

Blessed are the servants who don't regard themselves as better when they are esteemed and praised by others, than when they are accused as being as poor, ignorant, and despicable. For what we are in the sight of God is what we are—and no more!

Woe to followers who are elevated in reputation by others, but of their own will are not ready to be humbled. But blessed are those servants who are raised in dignity—not by their own will but by God—and who always desire to serve in humble ways.

Of Hiding Good Lest It Be Lost

Blessed are the servants who treasure up in heaven the good things which the Lord shows them and who don't wish to show them off to others with the hope of praise.

The Lord most high will display His works on whom ever He may please. Blessed are the servants who keep their good deeds as a secret in their heart—known only to the Lord.

Admonitions, Rules, Etc., Part 1

50

Serving Our Savior

Teresa of Avila

"The King will say to those on his right, 'Come, you who are blessed by my Father, inherit the Kingdom prepared for you from the creation of the world. For I was hungry, and you fed me. I was thirsty, and you gave me a drink. I was a stranger, and you invited me into your home. I was naked, and you gave me clothing. I was sick, and you cared for me. I was in prison, and you visited me.'

"Then these righteous ones will reply, 'Lord, when did we ever see you hungry and feed you? Or thirsty and give you something to drink? Or a stranger and show you hospitality? Or naked and give you clothing? When did we ever see you sick or in prison and visit you?'

"And the King will say, 'I tell you the truth, when you did it to one of the least of these my brothers and sisters, you were doing it to me!'"

Jesus, Matthew 25:34–40

I conclude briefly with this advice: do not build towers without foundations, for our Lord does not care so much for the importance of our works as for the love with which they are done. When we do all we can, His majesty will enable us to do more every day. We must not grow weary during the brief time this life lasts. (And perhaps it will be shorter than any of us think.)

We should give our Lord every sacrifice we can, both inwardly and outwardly. His majesty will unite these with what He offered to His Father for us on the cross, so that we may be worth the value lovingly given us, however meager the works themselves may be.

The Interior Castle, The Seventh Mansions, Chapter 4

51

Serving in the Spirit

Francis of Assisi

Feed the hungry,
and help those in trouble.
Then your light will shine out from the darkness,
and the darkness around you will be as bright as noon.

Isaiah 58:10

When I, Brother Francis, first began to live out my repentance, it seemed to me very bitter to serve lepers. But the Lord Himself led me among them, and I showed mercy to them. But when I left them, that which had seemed to me bitter was changed for me into sweetness of body and soul.

We should never desire to be above others, but rather to be servants and subject to every human creature for God's sake. And the Spirit of the Lord will rest upon all those who do these things and who persevere to the end. He will make His home and dwelling in them. They will be family of the heavenly Father, whose works they do. They are His spouses, brothers, and mothers of our Lord Jesus Christ. We are spouses when, by the Holy Spirit, our faithful souls are united to Jesus Christ. We are His brothers when we do the will of His Father who is in heaven. We are His mothers when we bear Him in our heart and in our body through pure love and a clean conscience. Then we will display Him by holy work which ought to shine as an example to others.

Testament of the Holy Father St. Francis

52

Surrendering to Service

Francis of Sales

For God is not unjust. He will not forget how hard you have worked for him and how you have shown your love to him by caring for other believers, as you still do.

Hebrews 6:10

I, the undersigned, in the presence of God and of all the company of heaven, renew my sacred promise of faithfulness to God made in my name at my baptism. I reject the devil, the world, and my earthly nature. I despise cursed temptations, pride, and lusts, now and for all eternity.

I have considered the infinite mercy of His heavenly goodness toward me, a most miserable, unworthy creature, whom He has created, preserved, sustained, delivered from so many dangers, and filled with so many blessings.

I have considered, above all, the incomprehensible mercy and lovingkindness with which this most good God has been merciful toward me in my sinfulness. He has led me so tenderly to repentance, and waited so patiently for me till this year of my life.

And turning to a loving and merciful God, I desire, intend, and deliberately resolve to serve and love Him now and eternally. I devote to His will all my mind and all its thoughts, my soul and all its powers, my heart and all its affections, as well as my body and all its senses.

I resolve never to misuse any part of my being by opposing His divine will and sovereign majesty. I wholly desire to sacrifice myself, vowing ever to be His loyal, obedient, and faithful servant without any change or recall.

But if unhappily, through the temptation of the Enemy or human weakness, I should in any way fail in my resolution and dedication, I most earnestly resolve by the grace of the Holy Spirit to rise up again as soon as I shall perceive my fall, and turn anew, without any delay, to seek His divine mercy.

This is my firm will and intention—my inviolable, irrevocable resolution—which I make and confirm without any reservation, in the holy presence of God, in the sight of the church triumphant, and before the church militant, which is my mother, who accepts this my declaration, in the person of Him who, as her representative, hears me make it.

Be pleased, O eternal, all-powerful, all-loving God—Father, Son, and Holy Spirit—to confirm me in this my resolution, and accept my hearty and willing offering. And as You have been pleased to inspire me with the will to make it, give me also the needed strength and grace to keep it. O God, You are my God, the God of my heart, my soul, and spirit, and as such I acknowledge and adore You, now and for all eternity. Glory be to Jesus. Amen.

Name ________________________________

Date ____________________________

Introduction to the Devout Life, Part 1, Chapter 20

VII

Suffering

We are pressed on every side by troubles, but we are not crushed. We are perplexed, but not driven to despair. We are hunted down, but never abandoned by God. We get knocked down, but we are not destroyed. Through suffering, our bodies continue to share in the death of Jesus so that the life of Jesus may also be seen in our bodies.

Second Corinthians 4:8–10

53. Bearing Christ's Cross: *Teresa of Avila*
54. Loving through Suffering: *Madame Guyon*
55. Becoming Intimate with Christ through Suffering: *John of the Cross*
56. Suffering with a Sweet Spirit: *Francis of Sales*
57. Following Christ's Example: *Thomas à Kempis*
58. Passing Through the First Dark Night of the Soul: *John of the Cross*
59. Passing Through the Second Dark Night of the Soul: *John of the Cross*
60. Praying for Intimacy with Christ: *Ignatius of Loyola*

53

Bearing Christ's Cross

Teresa of Avila

Then Jesus said to his disciples, "If any of you wants to be my follower, you must give up your own way, take up your cross, and follow me."

Matthew 16:24

To bear the cross of Christ, we must have a strong desire to suffer. Because our fervent wish is to identify with the suffering of Christ, troubles will not disturb our peace as before, for we are now content to suffer. We do not torment ourselves to death about it as we used to do.

We will feel a great inner joy when persecuted. It is far more peaceful than in the past when we were less willing to carry the cross. We bear no grudges against our enemies, nor wish them any harm. Indeed, we have a special love for them and deeply grieve when seeing them in trouble. We do all we can to relieve their suffering, earnestly interceding with God on their behalf. We should be glad to forfeit the favors our Lord shows us, so that they may be given to our enemies.

Most surprising to me in this work is this: The sorrow and distress of a person who wished she could just die and go be with the Lord, has been replaced with a fervent desire to serve and praise Him, and to help others with all her might.

We always find that those nearest to Christ our Lord bear the heaviest cross.

The Interior Castle, The Seventh Mansions, Chapter 3

I have known some, in fact numerous, souls who for many years have lived a regular well-ordered life both in body and mind. It would seem that they must have gained mastery over this world, or at least seem extremely detached from it. Yet, if His Majesty sends a very moderate trial, they become so disturbed and disheartened, that it not only astonishes me, but makes me anxious about them. Advice is useless to them. They have practiced the Christian faith for so long, they think they are capable of teaching it and believe they have abundant reason to feel miserable.

They believe their conduct is saintly, and wish others to agree with them. The only way to help them is to compassionately empathize with their troubles, since we can't help but feel sorry seeing people in such an unhappy state. However, they must not be argued with, for they are convinced they suffer only for God's sake, and can't be made to understand they are acting imperfectly. This happens to people who think they are so far advanced spiritually. No wonder that they should feel these trials for a time. God, wishing His children to realize how miserable spiritually they really are, often temporarily withdraws blessings. These trials prove to them in a very short time what they—and we—really are.

Trials and troubles quickly teach us! We perceive our faults very clearly. Sometimes the discovery of how quickly we are overcome by slight earthly trials is more painful than the subtraction of God's blessings. But God shows us great mercy in this way. For though our behavior may be lacking, we gain greatly in humility.

The Interior Castle, The Third Mansions, Chapter 2

54

Loving through Suffering

Madame Guyon

In his kindness God called you to share in his eternal glory by means of Christ Jesus. So after you have suffered a little while, he will restore, support, and strengthen you, and he will place you on a firm foundation.

First Peter 5:10

We may say we love Jesus, our Bridegroom. We may claim our love for Him is deep and strong, but is it really? Or do we take pleasure from the feelings of freedom and relief from the guilt of sin and the joy of forgiveness rather than in simply loving Him? Do we mourn when the pleasures of our Beloved are not felt? If so, it is our own satisfaction we seek. If we take pleasure in Jesus Himself, then we should rejoice in Him as much when we don't feel Him near as when we do. If not, our love is self-centered—not Christ-centered! We may believe we love Him for who He is, but do we love His blessing more than we love Him?

We may claim that we're willing to suffer for our Beloved, but only if He will take notice of it and make us feel His presence in it. We may say we desire no reward, but we take pains to make Him aware of our suffering and to approve of us. We want Him to take pleasure in us as we suffer. Oh, but how much we are deceived! Our jealous Lover will not permit us to enjoy the pleasure which we take in seeing His satisfaction with our sorrow. We must suffer without His appearing to see it, though of course He does. Anyone would be willing to suffer on such conditions, as it would give us a great gratification.

This is what it means to suffer deep in our souls: to feel our Beloved is unaware of our pain. To sense He despises what we do to please Him and turns away from it. To get the impression that what used to delight Him now prompts scorn. To see Him repay us with terrible coldness and distance as we passionately pursue Him and do all for His sake alone. To unjustly lose all He has given us as a promise of His love.

We ask, "Is this how we are repaid for our love, our faithfulness, and suffering without complaining?" To see others enriched with our work, but nevertheless continue to do what would please our absent Lover. We have not ceased to follow Him. And if we do stop for a moment, due to our unfaithfulness or something unexpected, we redouble our speed without thought or fear of falling. We will keep following our Lord, though we may fall a thousand times, till we are so weary that we lose our strength and die from continual fatigue.

If only our Beloved would turn and look upon us, His glance would restore life with the wonderful blessings it gives. But for now, He seems so cruel as to let us die without His help. This sense of abandonment by the Bridegroom may endure a long time, at least until our soul has made great advances in loving Him rather than His gifts. Unfortunately, many never reach this point in their spiritual journey.

Spiritual Torrents, Part 1, Chapter 5

55

Becoming Intimate with Christ through Suffering

John of the Cross

Jesus replied, "I tell you the truth, you want to be with me because I fed you, not because you understood the miraculous signs."

John 6:26

Christ is known very little by those who consider themselves His friends. We see them seeking in Him their own pleasures and comforts because of their great love for themselves. They don't love His bitter trials and His death, only His great love for them. These are those who consider themselves His friends, but they live far away in the world, withdrawn from Him, people of great learning and influence. They are ambitious for high places in society and the organized church. But, despite the good exterior, they don't know Christ, and their end will be very bitter.

Ascent of Mount Carmel, Book 2, Chapter 7

It is necessary for the soul, in order to become spiritually one with God, to pass through the dark night of the soul with its sacrifice of the desires and denial of pleasures in all things. This is because all earthly affections are pure darkness in the eyes of God. And when the soul is clothed in these desires, it has no capacity for being enlightened and possessed by the pure and simple light of God. Light cannot agree with darkness, since, as John writes, "The light shines in the darkness, and the darkness can never extinguish [or comprehend] it" (John 1:5).

Two opposite forces cannot coexist in one person. The darkness, which is desired by creatures, and light, which is God, are contrary to each other, and have no similarity or harmony between one another. As Paul taught the Corinthians: "Don't team up with those who are unbelievers. How can righteousness be a partner with wickedness? How can light live with darkness?" (2 Cor. 6:14). So, the light of divine union cannot dwell in the soul if these affections don't first flee away from it.

The love and attachments which the soul has for created things makes our soul like these creatures. And the greater the love and attachments, the more our soul becomes like them. For love creates a union and likeness between that which it loves and that which is loved. When we love a creature, we become as low as that creature, and, in some ways, lower; for love not only makes the lover equal to the object of his love, but even subjects him to it.

So, in the same way it comes to pass that the soul that loves anything else becomes incapable of pure union with God and transformation in Him. For the low estate of the creature is much less capable of union with the high estate of the Creator than is darkness with light. For all things of earth and heaven, compared with God, are nothing.

Ascent of Mount Carmel, Book 1, Chapter 4

56

Suffering with a Sweet Spirit

Francis of Sales

But Jesus said to them, "You don't know what you are asking! Are you able to drink from the bitter cup of suffering I am about to drink? Are you able to be baptized with the baptism of suffering I must be baptized with?"

Mark 10:38

Watch a bee hovering over the mountain thyme. The nectar it gathers is bitter, but the bee turns it all to honey. In the same way, as the faithful soul finds bitter herbs along its path of devotion, they are all turned to sweetness and pleasantness as it journeys. The martyrs have considered fire, sword, and rack as perfumed flowers because of their devotion. And if devotion can sweeten such cruel torments—even death itself—how much more will it give a charm to ordinary good deeds?

We sweeten unripe fruit with sugar, and it is useful in enhancing the taste of even good fruit. So devotion is the real spiritual sweetness which takes away all bitterness from earthly troubles, sickness, and death. Despite these earthly things, we have peace in our souls. It cures the poor of sadness and the rich of pride. It keeps the oppressed from feeling deserted and the prosperous from arrogance. It removes sadness from the lonely and indecency from our social life. It is as the sun's warmth in winter and refreshing dew in summer. It knows how to rejoice in abundance and to suffer in need, how to benefit from both honor and contempt, accepts gladness and sadness with a calm mind, and fills our hearts with a wondrous sweetness.

Introduction to the Devout Life, Part 1, Chapter 1

57

Following Christ's Example

Thomas à Kempis

Even though Jesus was God's Son, he learned obedience from the things he suffered.

Hebrews 5:8

The Christ
My children, I came down from heaven for your salvation. I took upon Myself your miseries, not of necessity, but motivated by love, that you may learn patience and might bear temporary miseries without complaining. For, since the hour of My birth until My death upon the cross, I didn't cease from bearing sorrow. I had a great lack of material things. I often heard many insults made against Me. I gently bore arguments and hard words. I received ingratitude for My benefits, blasphemies for My miracles, and rebukes for My doctrine.

The Disciple
Lord, in my life, You have been patient with me as You fulfilled the commandments of Your Father. So, it is well that I, a miserable sinner, should patiently bear my burden according to Your will as long as You

wish. I will bear with my salvation also the burden of this corruptible life. For although the present life seems burdensome, it is, however, made full by the work of Your grace. And to those of us who are weak, it becomes easier and brighter through the example of You and Your saints. Life is much more joyous than in ancient times under the Old Testament when the gate of heaven remained shut. Even the way to heaven seemed more obscure when so few cared to seek after the heavenly kingdom. But not even those who were righteous and following the way of salvation were able to enter the kingdom of heaven before Your passion and the ransom of Your holy death.

Oh, what great thanks I must give You for graciously showing me and all faithful people the good and right way to Your eternal kingdom. Your way is our way and, by holy patience, we walk to You, who are our crown. If You had not gone before and taught us, who would care to follow? Oh, how far would they have gone backward if they had not beheld Your glorious example! Behold, we are still lukewarm, though we have heard of Your many signs and teaching. What would become of us if we didn't have the light of the Spirit to help us follow You?

The Imitation of Christ, Book 3, Chapter 15

58

Passing Through the First Dark Night of the Soul

John of the Cross

Then Jesus turned to his disciples and said, "God blesses you who are poor, for the Kingdom of God is yours. . . . What sorrow awaits you who are rich, for you have your only happiness now."

Luke 6:20, 24

All the wisdom of the world and all human ability, compared with the infinite wisdom of God, are pure and supreme ignorance. As the apostle Paul writes, "For the wisdom of this world is foolishness to God" (1 Cor. 3:19). So, any soul that depends on its own knowledge and ability in order to gain the wisdom of God is supremely ignorant in the eyes of God and will remain far removed from His wisdom.

All the wealth and glory of all creation, in comparison with the wealth which is God, is supreme poverty and wretchedness. And so, the soul that loves and possesses earthly wealth is supremely poor and wretched in the sight of God. For that reason, it will be unable to attain to that wealth and glory which is the state of transformation in God.

Ascent of Mount Carmel, Book 1, Chapter 4

Stories and teachings from the Holy Scriptures prove how necessary it is for the soul to journey to God through a dark night of the death to the desire of all things.

And so, when our Lord marked the path for His followers, warned, "So you cannot become my disciple without giving up everything you own" (Luke 14:33). The Son of God came to teach contempt for all things, so we may receive the true reward of the Spirit of God in Himself. For, as long as the soul refused to reject all things—both earthly and spiritual—it has no capacity to receive the Spirit of God in pure transformation.

Ascent of Mount Carmel, Book 1, Chapter 5

How much greater is the work of God in the cleansing and the purging of a soul of unrighteousness than in the creating of that soul from nothing. For these contrary desires and affections are more completely opposed to God and offer Him greater resistance than does nothingness; for nothingness resists nothing at all.

- To have pleasure in everything, desire to have pleasure in nothing.

- To possess everything, desire to possess nothing.
- To be everything, desire to be nothing.
- To know everything, desire to know nothing.

In this detachment from earthly desires, the spiritual soul finds its quiet and rest. For since it covets nothing, nothing wearies it when it is lifted up, and nothing oppresses it when it is cast down, because it is in the center of its humility. But when it covets anything, at that very moment, it becomes wearied.

In the first dark night of the soul, we are deprived of these outward, earthly things.

Ascent of Mount Carmel, Book 1, Chapter 8

59

Passing Through the Second Dark Night of the Soul

John of the Cross

"Make sure that the light you think you have is not actually darkness."

Jesus, Luke 11:35

The second dark night of the soul is darker than the first. The first deals with our lower part, our sensual part, and consequently it's more exterior. But the second night, which is of faith, belongs to the higher part of us. This is the rational part and so is interior and more obscure, since it deprives us of the light of reason or to speak more clearly, blinds us. And so, it is appropriately compared to midnight, which is the deepest and darkest time of night.

Ascent of Mount Carmel, Book 2, Chapter 2

We are blinded toward God and spiritual things—our rational and higher part—in order that one may attain supernatural transformation. For this to happen, it is clear that we must be plunged into darkness. This transformation and union is something that cannot be comprehended by human ability and reasoning. Our soul must completely and voluntarily empty itself of all that can enter into it, whether from above or from below—anything its desire and will depend upon.

We must be like someone blind, leaning upon dark faith, taking it for a guide and light. In this night, we lean on nothing that we can understand, experience, feel, or imagine. All these things can cause us to stray as faith is above all that we can humanly understand, experience, feel, or imagine. And if we are not blinded by total darkness to earthly reason, we can't attain that which is greater—that which is taught by faith.

This is what the writer of Hebrews meant by "it is impossible to please God without faith. Anyone who wants to come to him must believe that God exists and that he rewards those who sincerely seek him" (11:6).

If we want to become joined in union with God, we must not walk by understanding, nor lean upon experience, feelings, or imagination. We must believe in His being, which is not perceptible to human understanding, desire, imagination, nor any other sense. It can't be fully known in this life. The highest thing that can be felt and experienced concerning God is infinitely remote from Him and the pure possession of Him. Paul writes, "That is what the Scriptures mean when they say, 'No eye has seen, no ear has heard, and no mind has imagined what God has prepared for those who love him'" (1 Cor. 2:9).

It is clear that, in order perfectly to attain to union with Christ in this life through grace and love, a soul must be in darkness with respect to all that can enter through the eye, and to all that can be received through the ear, and can be imagined with the mind, and understood with the heart. And so, our soul is greatly hindered from reaching this high estate of union with God when we cling to any human understanding, feeling, imagination, sight, will of its own, any other act, or to anything of its own. We must detach and strip ourselves of dependence on these things to obtain God who is beyond the highest thing that can be humanly known or experienced. And so our soul must pass through the second dark night to receive God's light.

The more our soul depends upon and builds up what can be understood, experienced, and imagined—whether it is spiritual or not—the more we lose the supreme good and the more we are hindered from attaining it.

When our soul is in darkness and blinded from all natural light, it will see supernaturally. When we depend upon any light of our own, we become blinder and come to a dead stop on our road to intimacy with Christ.

Ascent of Mount Carmel, Book 2, Chapter 4

Here is what happens when we experience human emptiness, darkness, detachment from all things—or spiritual poverty—all of which are one and the same. Our faith becomes ever more deeply rooted and infused in our soul. At the same time, the love of God also becomes rooted and infused in the soul ever more deeply. And so, the more we desire obscurity and sacrifice toward all the outward or inward things we can humanly receive, the more our soul is infused by faith, hope, and love, since these three godly virtues go together.

Ascent of Mount Carmel, Book 2, Chapter 14

The one and only reason for which God must be served is that He is who He is, and not for any other ulterior motive. And so, to serve Him for any other reason is to not serve Him.

Ascent of Mount Carmel, Book 3, Chapter 38

We become one with God, not by what we can humanly understand, perceive, feel, or imagine concerning Him. But, in purity and love, we reject and detach ourselves from everything that is not of God alone.

Ascent of Mount Carmel, Book 2, Chapter 5

60

Praying for Intimacy with Christ

Ignatius of Loyola

"I am in them and you are in me. May they experience such perfect unity that the world will know that you sent me and that you love them as much as you love me."

Jesus, John 17:23

Soul of Christ, sanctify me.
Body of Christ, save me.
Blood of Christ, inebriate me.*
Water from the side of Christ, wash me.
Passion of Christ, strengthen me.
O Good Jesus, hear me.
Within your wounds hide me.
Permit me not to be separated from you.
From the wicked foe, defend me.
At the hour of my death, call me
and bid me come to you
That with your saints I may praise you
*For ever and ever. Amen.***

*Or "overpower," if the original is a problem for teetotaling readers

**Note: This popular prayer is sometimes called Aspirations of St. Ignatius Loyola and appeared at the beginning of *The Spiritual Exercises of St. Ignatius of Loyola* as a preface for many years. However, its authorship is now considered uncertain.

Readings by Authors

Devotional Sources

The Ascent of Mount Carmel **by John of the Cross,** translated and edited by Edgar Allison Peers, from the edition of P. Silverio de Santa Teresa, 1934.

The Cloud of Unknowing **by Anonymous,** edited by Evelyn Underhill, John M. Watkins publisher, 1922.

The Dialogue of Saint Catherine of Siena **by Catherine of Siena,** translated by Algar Thorold, Kegan Paul, Trench, Trubner and Company publisher, 1907.

The Imitation of Christ **by Thomas à Kempis,** translated by William Benham, John C. Nimmon publisher, 1886.

The Interior Castle **by Teresa of Avila,** translated by the Benedictines of Stanbrook, Thomas Baker publisher, 1921.

Introduction to the Devout Life **by St. Francis of Sales,** M. H. Gill and Son publisher, 1885.

On Loving God **by Bernard of Clairvaux,** edited by Paul Halsall at Murray Fordham University. Online at https://www.ccel.org/ccel/bernard/loving_god.i.html.

Practice of the Presence of God: The Best Rule of Holy Life **by Brother Lawrence (Nicholas Herman),** edited by Edgar C Barton, The Epworth Press. Online at https://ccel.org/ccel/lawrence/practice/practice.i.html.

Revelation of Divine Love **by Julian of Norwich,** edited by Grace Warrack, Methuen and Company publishers,1901.

The Spiritual Exercises of St. Ignatius of Loyola translated Father Elder Mullan, S.J., P.J. Kennedy and Son publisher, 1914.

A Short Method of Prayer and *Spiritual Torrents* **by J.M.B. De La Motte Guyon,** translated by A.W. Marston; Sampson Low, Marston, Low, and Searle, 1875.

The Writings of St. Francis of Assisi, translated by Paschal Robinson, The Dolphin Press, 1905.

CLC PUBLICATIONS
Fort Washington, PA 19034

This book is published by CLC Publications, an outreach of CLC Ministries International. The purpose of CLC is to make evangelical Christian literature available to all nations so that people may come to faith and maturity in the Lord Jesus Christ. We hope this book has been life changing and has enriched your walk with God through the work of the Holy Spirit. If you would like to know more about CLC, we invite you to visit our website:

www.clcusa.org

To know more about the remarkable story of the founding of CLC International we encourage you to read

LEAP OF FAITH

Norman Grubb

Paperback
Size $5^1/_4$ x 8, Pages 248
ISBN: 978-0-87508-650-7
ISBN (*e-book*): 978-1-61958-055-8

The FAITHESSENTIALS Series

If you could recommend just one book other than the Bible, what would it be?

At CLC Publications, we strive to make sure that all the books we publish will help believers grow deeper in Christ, but there are some authors from across the centuries that stand apart.

Their works have such a universal message that they become essential reading for the Christian. Both timeless and timely, these classic writings have an approach to faith that is increasingly rare in our culture.

CLC's FaithEssentials Series is our attempt to bring these books together in a simple, attractive, and low-cost format that will allow you to add a growing number of classics to your bookshelf.

The **FaithEssentials Series** will include works from trusted authors like:

- Watchman Nee
- Thomas à Kempis
- John Bunyan
- Madame Guyon
- Bernard of Clairvaux
- A.W. Tozer
- John of the Cross
- Roy Hession

. . . and more!

Start collecting them now!

OTHER TITLES IN

The FAITHESSENTIALS Series

Sit, Walk, Stand

(with Study Guide)

by Watchman Nee

Paperback ISBN: 978-1-61958-316-0
Price: $5.99 | 111 pages

E-Book ISBN: 978-1-61958-027-5
Price: $8.99

An inspiring look at Ephesians, opening our eyes to the process of Christian living and maturity in three words: sit—our position in Christ; walk—our life in the world; and stand—our attitude toward the Enemy. New study guide included. An invaluable tool for the growing disciple.

OTHER TITLES IN

The FAITHESSENTIALS Series

The Pursuit of God

by A.W. Tozer

Paperback ISBN: 978-1-61958-312-2
Price: $6.99 | 157 pages

E-Book ISBN: 978-1-61958-313-9
Price: $3.99

"As a deer pants for flowing streams, so pants my soul for you, O God" (Ps. 42:1). Tozer seeks to make his readers thirsty for intimacy with the Creator, and inspires those who have found God to seek Him all the more passionately and intensely. Start your pursuit today!

OTHER TITLES IN

The FAITHESSENTIALS Series

The Calvary Road

by Roy Hession

Paperback ISBN: 978-1-61958-321-4
Price: $8.99 | 162 pages

E-Book ISBN: 978-1-61958-227-9
Price: $8.99

Do you long for revival and power in your life? Learn how Jesus can fill you with His spirit through brokenness, repentance and confession in this updated version of Hession's classic, The Calvary Road. In the course of eleven chapters, Hession emphasizes the need for personal revival in our life with Christ.